THE DISPOSSESSED

THE DISPOSSESSED

KARL MARX's Debates on Wood Theft and the Right of the Poor

DANIEL BENSAÏD

TRANSLATED AND WITH AN INTRODUCTION BY ROBERT NICHOLS

MIN
NE
SO
TA

UNIVERSITY OF MINNESOTA PRESS
MINNEAPOLIS
LONDON

The University of Minnesota Press gratefully acknowledges financial support for the publication of this book from the Centre national du livre.

The Dispossessed was originally published in French as *Les dépossédés: Karl Marx, les voleurs de bois et le droit des pauvres*. Copyright La fabrique éditions, 2007.

"Proceedings of the Sixth Rhine Province Assembly, Third Article" by Karl Marx was originally published in German in the supplement to *Rheinische Zeitung*, nos. 298, 300, 303, 305, and 307 (October 25, 27, and 30, November 1 and 3, 1842).

Published by the University of Minnesota Press
111 Third Avenue South, Suite 290
Minneapolis, MN 55401-2520
http://www.upress.umn.edu

ISBN 978-1-5179-0384-8 (hc)
ISBN 978-1-5179-0385-5 (pb)

Library of Congress record available at https://lccn.loc.gov/2020048338

Printed in the United States of America on acid-free paper

UMP BmB 2021

Contents

Crisis and Kleptocracy

Bensaïd for Our Times

ROBERT NICHOLS

We wanted a world in which the right to existence prevailed over the right to property, popular power over commodity dictatorship, the logic of needs over that of profits, public good over private egoism.

Daniel Bensaïd, *An Impatient Life*

This volume offers readers an unusual constellation of texts. In it, an essay from 2007 by the French philosopher Daniel Bensaïd is arranged alongside five short journalistic pieces by Karl Marx from the 1840s. While not exactly concentric to one another, these writings treat similar themes. In his journalism, we see Marx working through a clutch of concepts that would long occupy his intellectual and political agenda: property, theft, law, publicity, and the commons. Bensaïd's essay echoes these thematic concerns, explicitly building on Marx. At the same time, because the texts in question were originally written in different languages and composed more than a century and a half apart, a sequence of gulfs divides them in space, time, culture, and idiom. Therefore, in presenting these together here, this volume is intended as an experiment in arranging a series of reflections that share more than an overlapping set of substantive concerns; they might also be thought to model a mode of intervening into their respective eras. If the texts relate to one another effectively, it will not be because Bensaïd simply builds on Marx in the linear manner of layering or incrustation but rather because each thinker's writing works to perform an analogous function for its own period and context. Accordingly, they are offered here together not merely as a "collection" conventionally understood but as a deliberately asynchronic juxtaposition.

This introductory essay is intended to facilitate this critical juxtaposition. It is organized into three parts. I first provide a preliminary sketch of the major themes and lines of inquiry contained within these works. Second, because Daniel Bensaïd has only recently become well known to English-speaking audiences, I offer an overview of those details of his life and works that, in my estimation, will be most helpful to the uninitiated (including a list of translated and untranslated writings). Finally, I reflect more generally on this constellation of texts in terms of their critical utility for apprehending key features of our own time, with particular reference to what I will term *crises of kleptocracy.*

Context and Contributions

Daniel Bensaïd's essay "The Dispossessed" is succinct and clear enough to demand little by way of secondary exegesis. Even if this were not the case, it would be entirely unsuitable to offer commentary on the piece as if it were simply a contribution to political philosophy traditionally understood. After all, Bensaïd's essay—much like his oeuvre more generally—is not motivated by abstract speculation for its own sake. Rather, it emerges as a practical intervention into a concrete context, one in which the author is already situated and engaged. Accordingly, this section offers less an explication of meaning than a study of the essay's function as an intervention. To understand this requires grasping something of the political and intellectual context into which the essay is intervening, which is in turn facilitated by familiarity with the author and his times.

Bensaïd's essay was originally published in 2007, arriving just on the cusp of the largest global recession since the 1930s. In the years since, critical commentators have struggled to stabilize this chaotic period. Consider just some of the frequently cited narrative plot points: As the U.S. subprime mortgage bubble burst in mid-2007, it led to the rapid devaluation of mortgage-backed securities, a liquidity crisis among major U.S. banks, and a major drop in stock markets around the world. The U.S. federal government tried to stop the hemorrhaging by using public funds as a tourniquet. The Federal National Mortgage Association (Fannie Mae) and Federal Home Loan Mortgage Corporation (Freddie Mac) were directly taken over, while trillions of dollars—which might have been otherwise used for public goods and infrastructure projects—were employed to bail out major corporations such as Merrill Lynch and AIG. By 2009, problems had spread to the European Union, adding fuel to the sovereign debt crisis there. Once again, huge quantities of public funds were used to prop up the failing investment and banking firms that had sparked the crisis in the first place. Unemployment in some European countries exceeded 25 percent during this period. Beyond Europe and North America, the crisis manifested differently. In an attempt to shield themselves from the mercurial caprices of financial capital, transnational corporations and sovereign wealth funds alike went abroad in search of more stable investments in food and fuel. While massive spikes in prices on the consumer side of both commodities over the previous decade had already been pressing hard on the most vulnerable in the Global South, the global financial collapse did little to improve their plight. Even more ominously, the convergent effect of these processes fed into a wave of land grabs as powerful global actors sought an anchor in primary resource production. The impact on Africa was most dramatic. As the World Bank noted, the average annual expansion of land-acquisition projects by major corporations accelerated dramatically between 2008 and 2009, going from 4 to 56 million hectares. Moreover, "more than 70 percent of such demand has been in Africa; countries such as Ethiopia, Mozambique, and

Sudan have transferred millions of hectares to investors in recent years."[1] Observing these trends, many sounded the alarm of (neo) colonialism: yet another "scramble for Africa" was taking place.[2]

Critical commentary has struggled to locate these events within a coherent conceptual frame. What, if anything, unifies these otherwise disparate moments and locales? How ought they be conceptualized, in relation to one another and/or with respect to previous iterations of these phenomena? What vocabulary is appropriate for apprehending this dynamic, shifting, and, by some accounts, ongoing period of global capitalist crisis? For some, 2007–10 was another cycle in the "primitive accumulation of capital," first theorized by Marx in Part VIII of *Capital,* volume 1. For others, it was an instance of the "enclosures of the commons," a vocabulary radicalized and popularized by works such as E. P. Thompson's *Customs in Common* (1991), the writings of the Midnight Notes Collective, and, most recently, by Michael Hardt and Antonio Negri's trilogy of *Empire* (2000), *Multitude* (2004), and *Commonwealth* (2009).[3] Following David Harvey's lead, others preferred to speak of "privatization" and/or "accumulation by dispossession." This is part of the intellectual horizon on which Bensaïd's intervention is set, which is signaled in part by his use of the rather unusual term *les dépossédés* in the original title.

In some general sense, each of these frameworks expresses a long-standing desire to find a theoretical vocabulary appropriate for naming the enduring (albeit uneven and punctuated) logics of capital accumulation via the coercive seizure of public goods and assets, as distinct from accumulation via the regularized exploitation of waged labor. They returned to prominence in the first decade of the twenty-first century in part because that period demanded a language with which to name such recurrent events. And yet, these frameworks are also importantly distinct from one another. Because each of these provides a different basic idiom and set of archetypal metaphors, they compose irreducibly plural synchronic relations between disparate elements of the present. In their distinct linguistic and conceptual inflections, they suggest manifold cases, examples, and instances. At the same time, by implicitly or explicitly invoking different precedents, they also compose multiple genealogies and lineages backward into the past.

Bensaïd's essay "The Dispossessed" is a darkly prescient contribution to this shared field of analysis, but his voice and his methods are distinct. Rather than dwell entirely in the present crisis, his essay begins in an act of retrieval. He starts by returning us to the long history of these struggles and the theoretical apparatuses they have engendered. Specifically, "The Dispossessed" excavates Marx's early writings on the "theft of wood" as a means of launching a new examination into the rights of the poor, the idea of the commons, and the contemporary tensions inherent in private property as a social institution of mutual, yet asymmetrical, exclusion. Let us follow Bensaïd's lead and make a detour through Marx.

In Part I of "The Dispossessed," Bensaïd excavates new resources in the critical theory tradition for thinking about property, poverty, and power by providing us with a close reading of Karl Marx's early journalistic writings on the *Debatten über das Holzdiebstahlsgesetz,* or "debates concerning the laws on the theft of wood."[4] These understudied writings come from Marx's term working for the newspaper *Die Rheinische Zeitung,* a broadsheet launched in 1842 in the city of Cologne, Germany. The newspaper stood in an ambiguous and vexed relation to the Prussian state for the entirety of its short existence. On the one hand, it was originally conceived as a vehicle for Prussian governmental interests, specifically, as a bulwark against the rising discontent of the local Catholic population. Catholic discontent with Protestant Prussian rule had been rising throughout the region for some time. It had already led to the secession of Belgium from the Netherlands in 1830, for instance, and, in 1837–38, to the imprisonment of the archbishop of Cologne (Clemens August von Droste zu Vischering) for his promulgation of the doctrine of "ultramontanism," which elevated papal authority above secular rule. The older *Kölnische Zeitung* was the leading paper of the area and the primary vehicle for articulating and amplifying Catholic discontent in the context of this *Kölner Wirren* (Conflict of Cologne). Thus, when the *Rheinische Allgemeine Zeitung* was founded in 1841, it was intended to serve as a pro-Prussian, Protestant counterweight. The problem lay with finding the right figure to head this new paper.

Established business elites such as Georg Jun and Dagobert Oppenheim wanted the new paper to advance their interests and to defend the Prussian-dominated German customs union, or *Zollverein*. Accordingly, they initially sought out economic theorist Friedrich List to serve as editor. When he declined the position, they were forced to compromise with more radical backers such as Moses Hess, on whose recommendation Adolf Rutenberg was eventually hired. Rutenberg was already well acquainted with the "Young Hegelians"; he was Bruno Bauer's brother-in-law and a friend of Karl Marx. This was not what the Prussian establishment in Berlin had had in mind when they pushed for a new paper in Cologne. Instead of a pro-government propaganda tool, they ended up with a polemical critic run by socialists and Young Hegelians.

Even while living in Bonn at the time, a young Karl Marx (only twenty-four years old) began immediately contributing articles to the paper. In 1842, he provided two long essays. These essays combined two topics: the freedom of the press and the even more general issues of publicity and transparency in government.[5] The Prussian state had long engaged in all manner of censorship and suppression of a free press, which Marx railed against in his first essay. Then, in the second, he turned to the inadequacies of the local Rhineland Diet (Parliament). This legislative body was created by the Prussian government in the 1820s and was organized into various estates (higher nobility, lower nobility, town burghers, and peasants). Moreover, until the 1840s the Diets deliberated in secret, preventing the general populace from gathering even the most basic information about what was said or how matters were decided. Marx attacked the legal distinctions between social groups on which the idea of "estates" rested, but also, in a more unique and innovative move, linked this to the first matter (concerning freedom of speech) by arguing that both were about publicity and transparency. Above all, Marx attacked the idea that freedom was yoked to the particular privileges of social-group order, rather than being tied to the universal right of all.

The new broadsheet initially struggled to compete with its more established Catholic counterpart. Rutenberg's alcoholism and general ineptitude did nothing to aid its fortunes and he was pushed out of the editor's chair.[6] In October 1842, Marx was appointed to the editorial board in an attempt to bring fresh ideas to its pages. The rejuvenation effort worked. By January 1843, the *Rheinische Zeitung* boasted regular subscriptions in excess of three thousand, making it one of the mostly widely read and cited publications in the German-speaking world. Despite its apparent success—or perhaps because of it—the Prussian government under Friedrich Wilhelm IV was determined to have the paper suppressed. The irony was apparent to all: a journal that had originally been designed to advance the Prussian monarchy was now being shut down by it. After a struggle to keep the paper operating freely, Marx submitted his resignation as editor in March of that year. A few months later, he went into exile in Paris, where he started a new paper (the *Deutsch-Französische Jahrbücher*) through which he would eventually meet Friedrich Engels.

The most important essays Marx wrote during his tenure at the *Rheinische Zeitung* pertain to the debate of the Rhineland Diet on the alleged theft of wood by the rural peasantry. While Marx was living in the region, the Rhineland parliament sought to transform the forests of the province from a space of common access into a series of privately owned plots. Almost overnight, this had the effect of turning the rural peasantry—who had for centuries enjoyed feudal, customary rights to access the forests as a means of basic subsistence—into "thieves." It became illegal for peasants to so much as pick a stick of firewood or pluck an acorn off a branch and, if they did, they were obliged to compensate the forest owner for the lost value at a price estimated by the forester himself. At stake in this debate was not merely the specific problem of theft but the entire framework of customary law, property rights, and the movement to enclose "the commons" under way across Western capitalist countries. As Marx rightly noted at the time, the concept of property, and the fundamental organization of society that it expressed, were being transformed.

Marx's articles to the paper can only be described as journalistic in the loosest sense. Rather than short, descriptive pieces focused on local events, Marx tended to use events as springboards into long essays filled with dense theoretical reflection. As Gareth Stedman Jones puts it, Marx's "articles" "can best be understood as exercises in applied philosophy."[7] These writings have long languished in obscurity, particularly in the English-speaking world.[8] In the interests of revamping this work, the articles have been given a new, updated translation and reproduced here in their entirety.

Daniel Bensaïd recognized the theoretical importance of these early articles. Hence, Part I of "The Dispossessed" offers a systematic theoretical explication of Marx's original articles by, first, situating them in their historical and intellectual context. These writings are most often mined for their historical, rather than theoretical, significance. Specifically, they are commonly considered important as means of studying Marx's personal intellectual development. The time Marx spent in Cologne as editor of the *Rheinische Zeitung* is situated both geographically and chronologically between his Jena and Paris life, so it has long been of interest to understanding this transition. The period has been important to intellectual historians in plotting the nature and extent of Marx's break with Hegelian philosophy, moving him toward his own novel approach: the critique of political economy. Marx narrated the transition thus:

> In the year 1842–43, as Editor of the *Rheinische Zeitung,* I experienced for the first time the embarrassment of having

> to take part in discussions on so-called material interests. The proceedings of the Rhineland Parliament on thefts of wood, and so on . . . provided the first occasion for occupying myself with the economic questions.[9]

Engels later seconded this appraisal, stating that Marx's journalist works of this period were the vehicle that led him "from pure politics to economic relationships and so to socialism."[10] Engels also connected this period to Marx's later works through the theme of crisis.[11]

This would remain a piece of Marx's biographical trivia if it did not have larger theoretical implications. Hence, while Bensaïd confirms their narrative importance, he also moves beyond historical context and intellectual biography by demonstrating the linkages between these early works and Marx's more mature theoretical formulations in *Capital,* volume 1. Opening up to these broader questions is the function of Part II of "The Dispossessed." Bensaïd's intervention in this section demonstrates not only his philosophical acumen, but also his impressive range and ability to work across intellectual traditions. Here, the French philosopher engages numerous other thinkers—from the Putney debates to Locke, the Jacobins to Proudhon and Hegel—as he unfolds the more general question of dispossession and "property as theft." Most importantly, he links the Rhineland period to the long history of debates over the categories of "primitive accumulation," "enclosures of the commons," and, as the title itself attests, dispossession.

Bensaïd contributes to these theoretical debates not simply by offering more commentary on them, but by pushing the matter into the present. Part III turns decisively in this direction. If Marx can be said to have disclosed a set of contradictions at the heart of the modern conception of private property, the question remains how this might continue to guide us today. Here Bensaïd is at his most original and insightful. His turn to the present—and the future—is multifold. He first considers how contemporary developments in intellectual property, biotechnology, genomics, food security, and patent rights push the limits of our established conceptual frameworks. The fundamental paradox of private property as a social institution that enforces systemic exclusion remains at work, even while taking on new forms and valences in light of these recent developments. How, for instance, are we to conceive of a separation from the means of production when we are speaking of such abstractions as an idea, an innovation, or a new method? How does genome manipulation transform our commonplace conceptions of self-ownership? In tackling these questions, Bensaïd brings Marx beyond himself, and beyond the developments envisioned from the vantage of nineteenth-century industrial capitalism.

Despite the span of time separating his era from our own, in Bensaïd's hands Marx remains relevant to these debates because he provides us with a set of conceptual and methodological tools for unraveling the relationship between things, property, and law.

Consider, for instance, the seemingly odd preoccupation in Marx's articles with distinguishing between different kinds of wood. Why are the Rhineland legislators so concerned to differentiate the cutting down of living trees, the gathering of dead wood, and the picking of fruits of the forest (e.g., berries and acorns)? Marx understood that the preoccupation with supposed ontological differences between things actually revealed a deep anxiety about the relation between the natural and the artificial, which in turn hinged upon the status of human labor. Labor is the name for the process that transforms the raw material of nature into the artifacts of the human world.[12] If property right is indexed to the transformative activity of labor (as Locke would have it), then it will be necessary to discern its precise contributions. Because the Rhineland Parliamentarians were anxious to defend their own acts of enclosure while at the same time limiting the rights of the poor, they were consumed by the problem of differentiating the labor involved in each. (Hence the lengthy commentary on green versus dead wood in the articles to follow: from the standpoint of pseudo-Lockean desert theories of property, one must carefully preserve the difference between collecting dead branches versus cutting down a living tree.) For Marx, however, the endemic difficulty in stabilizing the categorical distinctions between kinds of objects reveals a deeper crisis of the laboring subject. The transformative acts of labor can only generate a private right of property if in the first instance that labor is securely "my own." As Marx would argue in later writings, however, the very idea of a self-contained and self-possessed laboring subject is specious: all labor is social. It follows from this that the entire project of assigning property according to the meritorious actions of discrete individuals is a conceptual fiction and a political or ideological tool.

In Bensaïd's context (and our own), this anxiety about the ontological status of different kinds of objects—the "natural" and the "artificial"—is transposed into the problem of distinguishing between "invention" and "discovery." This has likewise generated a series of conceptual and legal contortions, which Bensaïd explores. This is clearest in the field of intellectual property. If a patent holder wishes to claim exclusive rights over an idea or a technique of genetic manipulation, for example, then she must demonstrate the precise extent of her original, creative contribution. Doing so requires erecting a barrier between the thing in its "natural condition" and the resultant transformation. This turns out to be highly unstable, however, because the object in its "natural state" is almost invariably the product of previous rounds of transformations by others. Thus, the new patent claim does not arise ex nihilo; it is an act that expropriates from someone else's prior right. By its own logic, the patent appears to secure the private property rights of some only by violating those of others. Property destroys property. Although the modern intellectual property claim presents itself as if it picks fruit from the free tree of nature, it rather invades a cultivated forest and removes our shared timber.

A final topic concerns the law. As both Marx and Bensaïd point out, law does not function here as a neutral arbiter of equal claims. Rather, it generates a false image of formal equality of right in order to mask the substantive inequalities it produces and defends. Marx put this point in a more elaborated form in "On the Jewish Question," where he wrote:

> The state abolishes, after its fashion, the distinctions established by *birth, social rank, education, occupation,* when it decrees that birth, social rank, education, occupation are *non-political* distinctions; when it proclaims, without regard to these distinctions, that every member of society is an *equal* partner in popular sovereignty, and treats all the elements which compose the real life of the nation from the standpoint of the state. But the state, none the less, allows private property, education, occupation, to *act* after *their* own fashion, namely as private property, education, occupation, and to manifest their *particular* nature.[13]

In the context of the enclosures, we might add "criminal status" to this list of enumerated social distinctions. For here, the law functions to authorize the simultaneous seizure of public goods and criminalization of those who would resist this act of dispossession. As Bensaïd puts it, "Judicial quantification is presented as a system of equivalence and proportion between crime and punishment."[14] As a mode of abstraction, the law appears to offer formally equal recognition to the property rights of all and, conversely, an equal threat of criminalization for violations of those rights. However, by failing to account for the extralegal and coercive origins of property right, the law actually functions to secure the asymmetrical domination of the few over the many. The peasants are cast as thieves of *wood* only by virtue of the fact that the wealthy burghers have already stolen *the woods* themselves. We need the expanded view of critical theory to help us see the forest for the trees.

This dimension of Bensaïd's analysis is indebted and contributing to another background debate: Marxist theories of law. First outlined by Evgeny Pashukanis in his *General Theory of Law and Marxism* (1924), the category of law was given further elaboration in the French context by Louis Althusser and Nicos

Poulantzas in particular.[15] They were in direct conversation with English theorists such as Ralph Miliband and have been picked up by later thinkers on the Continent, such as Pierre Lascoumes, Paul Sereni, Hartwig Zander, and Mikhail Xifaras, each of whom has also reached back to the Rhineland articles as resources for a reconstruction of the relation between law, property, and power.[16] Bensaïd contributes something novel to these debates by considering how, in the contemporary context, law increasingly projects into the future. He does so through his observation that new property regulation and, in particular, patent legislation represents not merely an enclosure of new kinds of objects and novel technologies, but of the very *expectation of benefit* derived from them. Patent holders lay claim to any possible future benefits derived from new inventions and, in this way, they stamp knowledge production processes themselves with exclusive ownership prior to the arrival of any particular new innovations. Thus, they enclose the future itself.[17] Bensaïd grasps the novel logic of these contemporary processes and yet, by connecting them back to Marx's writings on the theft of wood, he also successfully frames the underlying continuities and persistent challenges of private property and capitalist accumulation. In this way, "The Dispossessed" brilliantly works back and forth across time to disclose both continuity and rupture in our relationships to property and, through it, to one another.

In a short piece such as "The Dispossessed," a number of lines of inquiry must remain in the background, relatively unexplored or underexamined. To my mind at least, two stand out most pertinently. First, while Bensaïd (and Marx before him) recognized the necessarily expansionist tendencies of capital accumulation, there is little sense given here of how to relate different temporal–spatial conjunctures of capital and empire. As the brief biographic sketch below will attest, Bensaïd was a lifelong Trotskyist who did considerable organizing work in Latin America. He was, therefore, thoroughly immersed in the debates over "uneven and combined development." The question of empire and colonialism is periodically referenced in "The Dispossessed"—for instance, in the reference to "colonial appropriation of lands decreed 'virgin'" (Bensaïd, Part I, "Hybrid and Uncertain Property")—but not given a full treatment. The absence of a more elaborated discussion in this particular essay may, therefore, be driven by a need to narrow the aperture of investigation. The task of relating this particular context of dispossession to others globally via the articulation of capital accumulation and racial governance, colonialism, and imperialism remains all the same. Other works by Bensaïd (listed in the select bibliography at the end of this book) might be used to supplement this essay on this front.

A second and related question persists with regard to the agency of the "dispossessed" themselves. While Bensaïd, his predecessors, and his interlocutors provide a number of tools for understanding the coercive seizure of public goods and assets under the rubric of "primitive accumulation," "enclosures," or "dispossession," they do not always offer a concomitant account of the forms of agency and resistance this engenders. Despite the title of his essay, Bensaid's focus here is principally on *dispossession,* not the *dispossessed.* To think the latter would require delving into the long-standing debate within critical theory of various stripes concerning the status of those subjects who have not been integrated into the wage-labor system. Rendered superfluous, they experience capitalism not as a condition of exploitation, but of abandonment, exile, and death. Marx and Engels may have doubted the revolutionary potential of this "lumpenproletariat," but numerous lines of Marxist thought since their time have complicated and corrected this apparent dismissal. Moreover, such populations have almost always played a central role in anticolonial Marxism: from Mao and Ho Chi Minh on the peasantry to Frantz Fanon's wretched of the earth. Today, a strand of this debate has been resurrected in work on the precariate and in Foucauldian-inflected studies on the necropolitics of racialized "surplus" populations.[18] At stake in each of these iterations is the question of how to theorize collective agency and resistance in a context of extreme deprivation and marginalization. The structure of power and agency is distinct from the one imagined to obtain between, say, the bourgeoisie and the proletariat because the latter classic oppositional pairing is dialectically interrelated in a manner that cannot be easily transposed to other categories. In its classical iteration, the revolutionary potential of the proletariat is thought to reside in a certain leverage capacity it exercises over the capital relation itself by virtue of being paradoxically both subordinated and yet fundamental to its material reproduction. This cannot be said of the rural peasants in Southeast Asia, Indigenous peoples of the Americas, or the racialized slave classes of the world whose lives have been rendered expendable or, what is even worse, obstacles to natural resource extraction and development projects.[19] When your body is not even wanted as a tool of exploitation, what leverage do you have over the machinery of power? Where does that leave the agency of the dispossessed in relation to the forces aligned against them? Again, for a full treatment of such themes we would need to look beyond the confines of this one essay.

Ultimately, if we are to remain faithful to the spirit of critique embodied in the analysis given by Bensaïd and Marx, respectively, then we must appropriate them *for our own time*. But what is our own time and in what way does it relate to theirs? The question is immeasurably complex. In one sense, of course, our current era is a continuation of the one into which Bensaïd's essay was intervening. Far from the much prophesied "end of history," the twenty-first century has thus far been one of intense contradiction and convulsion. Reactionary ideologies once thought safely laid to rest have joined forces with predatory kleptocracy. If it has ever been possible to distinguish neatly the political, economic, and ecological fields of contestation, such distinctions are rapidly collapsing. The scope of the struggle is planetary and the stakes are nothing less than the conditions of life itself.

Within this conflagration, logics of dispossession have taken center stage. As I have argued elsewhere, dispossession might be thought here as both creative and destructive: a process that creates its own objects of appropriation.[20] Wider and wider communities are being drawn into dispossession's orbit as we find that it is indeed possible to lose that which we did not even know we "had" to begin with: earth, air, water, ideas, words, personal identity . . . the list goes on. Bensaïd sharpens our eye on the stakes of this. As he puts it in his autobiography:

> The generalised privatization of the world cannot be limited to commodities, goods, and services. It inexorably extends to the privatization of violence, the abolition of the state monopoly on its legitimate exercise, the dissemination of its means and the proliferation of 'irregular' actors (militias, armed bands, mafias). The deliberately confused presentation in imperial rhetoric of an obscure and ungraspable terrorism bases itself on these very real tendencies in order to build on fear and anxiety, the vision of a world under assault from barbarians. It masks the fact that this barbarism is in no way foreign to civilisation, being rather its reverse and inverse side. It is *its* barbarism.[21]

If we are to resist and transcend the barbarism of the present, we will require both diagnostic tools and utopian alternatives. While Bensaïd provides us with more of the former than the latter, his energy and acumen drive us forward into a future in which the struggle will increasingly be led by "the dispossessed."

A second-order problem we face with respect to these struggles is that it has already become a cliché to define our era as one of crisis. Climate change. Authoritarian populism. Yawning inequality. Mass migration and refugee displacement. Violence, terrorism, wars without end. The twenty-first century has seen an expanding and interlocking range of serious challenges to global social, political, and economic order. It is not simply that one struggles to determine *which* crisis is determinant—causally, normatively, or otherwise. Rather, in such a context, the concept of crisis itself can easily become overworked and depleted of its critical powers to name an exception. The danger is: where everything is a crisis, then it seems that nothing is.

We are helped here by the fact that Bensaïd thought deeply and seriously about the nature of crisis and the impoverishment of language that it can engender. Particularly in the late years of his life, Bensaïd worked extensively with major texts by Marx and Lenin to develop a unique account of crisis, situating the concept in relation to a host of proximate terms in that tradition: contradiction, interruption, break, opportunity, revolution.[22] Above all, however, Bensaïd drew from Walter Benjamin in the composition of a novel investigation into the vagaries of "crisis" as category of analysis. Benjamin had, of course, already turned the notion on its head when he insisted that, viewed from the "tradition of the oppressed," the emergency situation was already the rule, the exception was the norm.[23] Bensaïd recognized that this radically reoriented the very notion of crisis by challenging the linear, progressive philosophy of history on which it too often rested.[24] Dispensing with the homogeneous, empty time of modernist theories of historical progress, and embracing the Benjaminian concept of "now-time" *(Jetzzeit),* Bensaïd sought to renew the concept of crisis by repoliticizing it. For if there is no objective, "scientific" philosophy of history, then there is likewise no stable referent by which to determine the relative exceptionalism of the present, and the naming of the crisis becomes itself partisan. It is not a matter of *whether* or *which,* but crisis *for whom?* Perhaps most uniquely, Bensaïd modeled Benjaminian reflection on temporality and crisis in the very form of his address. As Enzo Traverso has argued, rather than offer commentary on Benjamin, in effect, Bensaïd treated the great German-Jewish thinker anachronistically, that is, as a contemporary who could speak across times. As Traverso puts it, "Bensaïd stressed the revolutionary dimension of Benjamin's messianic thought. Departing from a linear conception of time, he recognized the *kairotic* rhythm of history, that is, an asynchronic, 'discordant' rhythm, permanently opened to the irruption of event. He did not believe in historical teleology and, as we have seen, he considered struggle to be the only predictable thing."[25] By directly wresting Benjamin for his own time, the form of Bensaïd's work further reflected its thematic focus on contretemps and nonlinearity.

Bensaïd referred to Benjamin as a messianic watchman.[26] Perhaps we can treat Bensaïd himself in like fashion.[27] The form of asynchronic juxtaposition exhibited by this volume is intended to facilitate such treatment, for, again, our primary aim here need not necessarily be to retrieve the contributions of Marx and Bensaïd directly for the present. Instead, we might also ask how they assist us to critically intervene in our time as they did in theirs. This would require searching out formal and functional analogies rather than substantive homologies.

Consider: Marx and Bensaïd are both concerned with specific instances of enclosure, appropriation, and theft. They likewise share a second-order concern with how hegemonic modes of narrating injury and redress structure these first-order struggles. In this way, their work exhibits formal similarities across the substantive differences in the relevant forms of property at stake in their respective periods: from fallen wood to gene patents. Preserving the critical thrust of these insights prompts us not only to ask what new objects have become objects of dispossession in our present moment (from personal identity to outer space, the frontiers of appropriation appear limitless and elusively receding), but also how this has become a governing rationality for our age. If wider and wider swaths of humanity can be plausibly figured as the dispossessed, it speaks to the rise of kleptocracy as a governing rationality at a scale beyond even that envisioned by the nineteenth or twentieth centuries. And yet, the *form* of their respective critical interventions also cautions us against too easily adopting the dominant vocabulary of our period. Seen from this vantage, the shared concern with the *kleptocratic* dimension of contemporary problems might be thought of as symptomatic of the profundity of our crisis.[28] Does it not already speak to the transformation of our conceptual vocabulary that we cannot but articulate our experience of these events in terms of theft, that is, as an attack on our rights as *owners* rather than, say, citizens of a *demos*? Does this not already implicate us in an idiom of possession, ownership, and fealty to law? More generally, what does it say about the pervasiveness of neoliberal economic rationality that it has become difficult (if not impossible) to critique these processes in a language that is not already "indebted" to them?[29] If we are to apprehend this linguistic and conceptual field itself, we will need some vantage from which to view it. Moving outside our time, approaching it on the oblique—that is, via a situation that is neither entirely foreign, nor reducible to, our own—will be necessary. Hence asynchronic juxtaposition.

Biography

Daniel Bensaïd's intellectual contributions are inextricably intertwined with his personal development and political commitments. One cannot understand the former without the latter. This isn't due to an overdetermination by biography and context. Rather, it is a function of a deliberate, studied practice of integration, a result of the work of aligning the concentric circles in which the self is nested, from the intimate to the local, national, and global. The language of the "public intellectual" once served as a proxy for one face of this. Today this terminology is too tightly associated with an outdated hagiographic approach to intellectual history—there is no "Saint Daniel" here. At the same time, it is a language that has been abused by a culture of self-commodification and personal branding. As such, it is paradoxically too lofty and too debased to be of much utility here. It is perhaps best to stay close to the specific terminology Bensaïd himself wrestled with: the *intellectuel engagé*. As he articulated the term in his autobiography:

> So much has been said about 'committed intellectuals'. If a distinction can still be made between those 'working on things' and those 'working on thought', then the term may

be acceptable. On condition, of course, that the asymmetry of their relationship is not forgotten. In the social division of labour, theoretical knowledge and the manipulation of language play an important role, but there is no human activity that does not involve the intervention of thought. The non-intellectual does not exist.[30]

Bensaïd's status as an *intellectuel engagé* has even been retroactively attributed to his emergence on the French political scene in his role as a young student in the dramatic events of May 1968. As we shall see, this was only one small episode in a lifelong commitment to emancipatory struggle. Thus, unlike many others associated with the period, Bensaïd was reluctant to concede to its many myths. As he put it: "[E]nough harking back to 1968, enough generational effusions, memories of youthful companionship at the finest age of life. Too much has been said and too much made . . . We were not born to political action in '68, and we are not hostages of this imaginary birth."[31] Perhaps therefore, it is best to begin not with this "imaginary birth," but with his literal one.

Daniel Bensaïd had a pugnacious provenance. His mother, Marthe (née Starck), came from a long line of working-class communists, extending back to the Paris Commune. At the age of eighteen, she moved from the small city of Blois in central France to Oran in northwest Algeria. There she met Haïm Bensaïd, a Sephardic Jew and welterweight boxing champion. The two scandalized locals with their courtship and marriage, living together in Oran until the war crashed down on their world. With the capitulation of France to Germany in 1940, Haïm was sent to Drancy internment camp to await deportation to Auschwitz. Although Haïm escaped death at the hands of the Nazis, his two brothers did not.

When Daniel was born in Toulouse in 1946, he entered a familial and national context that was already intensely politicized along multiple lines. The horrors of the Nazi regime had hardly subsided when the French–Algerian war brought conflict back home. Schoolyard bullies had already made it clear that he could never be "truly French" but, by sixteen, he had embraced the critical exteriority this implied as a political identity. When French police massacred pro-National Liberation Front (FLN) members in October 1961 and again in February 1962, the then sixteen-year-old Bensaïd responded by joining the Union des étudiants communistes (UEC) and, along with several schoolmates, founding the Jeunesse Communiste group at his lycée.

Even within the communist left of his youth, Bensaïd remained a critical contrarian. In 1966 he moved to Paris to begin studies at the prestigious École normale supérieure in Saint-Cloud. Almost immediately, he and his peers began agitating the senior leadership of the Parti communiste français (PCF). Linkages between the national and international stage of struggle were becoming clearer, yet were polarizing and fracturing the left. The Sino–Soviet conflict loomed large, as did the Havana Declaration. Che Guevara had just delivered his famous speech at the Afro-Asian Conference in Algiers (February 1965) and published *Socialism and Man in Cuba* (March 1965). At the congress of the Union des étudiants communistes in Nanterre in 1966, Bensaïd and his Jeunesse Communiste group pressed all these issues to the fore. They challenged the PCF leadership on multiple fronts. On theoretical grounds, they questioned Stalinism and dared to quote Trotsky and Luxemburg. On the policy front, they denounced the PCF's support for Mitterrand in the 1965 election, its lukewarm backing for the Vietnamese, and its belated support for the Algerian FLN. As a result, they were effectively expelled for their heresy, leaving that year to form the Jeunesse Communiste Révolutionnaire (JCR).[32] The name was a provocation and a statement: the traditional parties, including the Communist Party, had lost the youth. The JCR was predominately led by young men in their twenties such as Alain Krivine, Henri Weber, and Gérard Verbizier. Bensaïd himself was only twenty at the time.

On an organizing level, the main lines of division in France were then between the JCR and the Maoists. Some combination of Che, Trotsky, and Henri Lefebvre helped inoculate Bensaïd against what he later termed the "religious cult of the red proletarian" that had arisen around Stalin and Mao, respectively.[33] These political battles were attended by intellectual ones. Sartre had dominated the left intelligentsia for a full generation already, but his hegemony was giving way. Althusser's *For Marx* arrived in 1965 as a direct challenge to the existentialists. It was followed soon after by *Reading Capital* (1968). Bensaïd and his peers gravitated more toward the nonconformist theorizing of Lefebvre, with whom Bensaïd completed his *maîtrise,* writing on Lenin's theory of revolutionary crisis.

As tumultuous as 1966–67 had been, in retrospect it appeared as mere "prehistory."[34] In February 1968, Bensaïd traveled to Berlin to participate in protests and demonstrations against the war in Vietnam, which generated repression and clashes with the police. Learning from this experience of direct action, on his return to France Bensaïd cofounded (with Daniel Cohn-Bendit) the Mouvement du 22 Mars in Nanterre. Expressly anti-imperialist (in solidarity with those in Indochina and Latin America), anti-bureaucratic (in solidarity with Polish student uprisings and the Prague Spring), and, of course, anticapitalist, the 22 of March Movement was the spark that ignited a powder keg. In May 1968, the Sorbonne was occupied. Bensaïd was thrown into the heart of the struggle: he spoke at the Mutualité on May 9, 1968. The next day, he and fellow student activists were overturning cars and using chainsaws to bring down trees along the boulevards to erect barricades. A spreading social rebellion followed suit. May 13 brought more than a million people to the streets in support of a general strike called by the communist-led Confédération générale du travail (CGT). By June, approximately ten million workers, or two-thirds of the French workforce, were directly engaged in strikes and occupations. The de Gaulle regime fought back with waves of arrests and police brutality. The JCR found itself outlawed, its leadership under continuous threat of imprisonment. Like close comrades Alain Krivine (born 1941), Henri Weber (born 1944), and Guy Hocquenghem (1946–88), Bensaïd went into hiding. He spent most of that summer sheltered by legendary writer and film director Marguerite Duras (1914–96).

Although he found himself at the heart of one particular eruption, Bensaïd never failed to recognize that this was a global battle with multiple epicenters. Paris, Berlin, Prague, Tlatelolco square, Tommie Smith and John Carlos, My Lai, the fall of Ayub Khan . . . the key names and sites are too numerous to list in any but the most cursory manner. Much mythologized and endlessly debated, volumes of work have already been produced on the events of 1968 and no attempt will be made here to summarize them. Insofar as it is necessary for understanding his intellectual and political development, it is worth noting that Bensaïd decisively rejected dominant interpretations of that fateful year. One such discourse would reduce it to a "generational drama," that is, a revolt of the youth against their elders. Another would subsume its conflicts beneath the *longue durée,* plotting them, for instance, as the culmination of developments begun in 1848 or even 1789. A third (attributed by Bensaïd to Alain Badiou) was that of the "fetishised hypostasis." This reduced May '68 to a quasi-theological moment, "something that happens by excess, beyond all calculation."[35] For Bensaïd, each of these conspired to neutralize the importance of that year by stripping it of its essentially *political* character. These narratives deflect and defer questions of tactics and strategy—the years of building collective capacity—and thereby dissolve the political dimension into the psychological, sociological, and theological, respectively.[36]

The 1970s realigned forces into new projects, relationships, and political configurations. In 1970–71, Bensaïd did his Certificat d'aptitude au professorat de l'enseignement de second degré (CAPES) and was assigned to teach in Condé-sur-Escaut, a tiny town that had "scarcely been touched by the earthquake of 1968."[37] He remained close to his organizing comrades through frequent trips to Paris or common excursions into fascist Spain to help comrades fighting the Franco regime. On one such trip, he met Sophie Oudin, whom he would eventually marry.

Of course, the European left of the 1960s was not organized

along a single axis. Race, gender, sexuality, nationality, and other modes of social-group identification mattered. Fitting these together into a coherent whole was a struggle, as much then as today. Friendships were tested. For example, in 1969, Bensaïd's friend and confidant Guy Hocquenghem was expelled from the Ligue Communiste. The latter would go on to join Vive la révolution! (VLR), a group that distinguished itself from the more purist Maoist militants of the Gauche prolétarienne by its interest in gender and sexuality, the American counterculture, and immediate experiments in lifestyle politics (one meaning behind its name).[38] By 1971, Hocquenghem had also become a leading member of the FHAR (Homosexual Front for Revolutionary Action), which was likewise defined by its visceral opposition to the PCF and, more generally, to the felt puritanism of the French left.[39]

More directly relevant to Bensaïd was his Jewish heritage. Just one year after the JCR was founded, the Six-Day War put them to the test. The War of Attrition and the Yom Kippur War polarized and fractured the left, forcing all those of conscience to choose sides. Bensaïd resisted the pull of Zionist nationalism that drew many away from the Communist parties. As he put it in a retrospective moment:

> From being intransigent against anti-Semitism, we now came out as resolutely anti-Zionist, deeply convinced that, far from being incompatible, the two things went together. Refusing to accept the pariah status of the Palestinians essentially meant remaining faithful to the history of Jewish suffering.[40]

Bensaïd subsequently wrote with some ambivalence about his own Jewishness. His last two books, *Fragments mécréants* (An unbeliever's discourse) and *Éloge de la politique profane* (In praise of secular politics), are both highly critical of "identity politics," as it would eventually be known in Anglophone circles.[41] In 1982, he demonstrated against the Lebanese war; the siege of Beirut and massacres at Sabra and Shatila further clarified his allegiances.

The decade that followed produced a series of victories that, paradoxically, also brought irrelevance. The dictatorships in Greece, Portugal, and Spain fell but quickly transitioned to capitalist societies. The European Communist parties had some of their greatest electoral successes (in 1976, the Italian Communist Party rivaled the Christian Democrats and threatened to supplant them), but they were not able to articulate a lasting vision of a postcapitalist society. In France, the *soixante-huitard* moment was slowly absorbed into the political and cultural elite, stabilizing the status quo rather than undermining it. The revolutionary students became professors. The organizers joined the government but did not fundamentally change it.

During this period Bensaïd began to reorient his political cartography, turning to Latin America for its energy and innovation.[42] He made his first trip to the region in 1973, at a time when the whole Southern Cone was in upheaval. In Chile, the Pinochet coup had just detonated, sending shockwaves throughout the continent. The dictatorship was crumbling in Argentina and Juan Perón was waiting in the wings for his return. Juan María Bordaberry was in the process of installing a newly organized junta in Uruguay, while Brazilians were struggling against an old one. Over the whole of the decade, the U.S.-backed "Operation Condor" program of assassinations, coups, torture, and repression cut a bloody swath across the region. Close proximity to Latin American struggles in the 1970s led Bensaïd to reevaluate his political commitments, principles, and tactics. The question of violence was paramount. As he put it in his autobiography:

> My initiatory visit to Argentina inoculated me against an abstract and mythical view of armed struggle. I saw that weapons did not draw an unbridgeable border between reform and revolution, and that there could be an armed reformism: the long history of Latin American populism offers several examples. Under the impact of the Cuban revolution, it was possible for armed struggle to appear as a watershed. Yet it could never define a strategy. Protracted people's war, armed

insurrection, armed propaganda: a number of different projects and practices could hide under the same words.[43]

From then on, Bensaïd was considerably less sanguine about the followings that had arisen around Stalin, Mao, and even Che. He would subsequently always insist on the need to differentiate more carefully the validity of armed struggle from the "deadly nihilism" of those who would erect "death into a supreme sacrificial virtue."[44]

The role of violence in general, and guerrillas specifically, was front and center at the Tenth World Congress of the Fourth International in 1974. After participating in this debate, Bensaïd worked to transform the Jeunesse Communiste Révolutionnaire (JCR) into the Ligue Communiste Révolutionnaire (LCR), which would remain the leading party of the far left in France until the 2000s. Two years later, he attended the founding congress of Lotta Continua, the largest organization of the extraparliamentary left in Europe at the time. Simultaneously, he was working to support the Revolutionary Workers' Party (PRT) in Mexico.[45] In the lead-up to the 1978 French legislative elections, growing tensions between the Socialist and Communist parties meant that they were not able to update their *Programme commun*. The right continued to exploit that division and, for the first time since 1936, the Socialists outperformed the Communists. This signaled the turning of a tide in the West. Margaret Thatcher and Ronald Reagan were lurking around the corner.

Polish strikes in 1981 through to the fall of the Berlin Wall in 1989 revealed how rapidly the communist bloc was transforming. By that point, the memory of 1968 was no longer about the contradictions of capitalism but about a moment of cultural transition: the rebellious youth had pushed France toward modernization (however misguided they had been), which the new neoliberal movement would complete. Together they would defeat "the archaisms of a centralising Jacobin state, the hypocrisies of an outdated moral code, and the rigidity of established social hierarchies."[46] Mitterrand was enjoying a second term. The "New

Philosophers" rose to fame, denouncing the excesses of the past and reframing the question as one not of class struggle or imperialism but of "totalitarianism versus democracy." They became the theoretical voice of the neoliberal counterreform of the 1980s.

On the international stage, Third Worldism was collapsing and giving way to disillusionment. In 1980, Bensaïd visited both the United States and Brazil for the first time. He saw more hope in the southern continent than the northern. Between 1980 and 1990, he visited Brazil two or three times per year. He helped to launch the Partido dos Trabalhadores (PT) in 1980, which would go on to serve as one of Brazil's main ruling parties to the present day. Latin American struggles of the 1980s yielded mixed results. Military dictatorships in Brazil, Uruguay, and Argentina fell, but Operation Condor was still a brutal force and, by the close of the decade, the "double electoral defeat of the Sandinistas in Nicaragua and Lula in Brazil closed this promising cycle."[47]

The early 1990s ushered in a wave of Euro-markets and Euro-currencies, which were met by a series of protests, marches, revolts, and demonstrations. Mass strikes against neoliberal austerity politics in France in 1995 foreshadowed the failure of the Multilateral Agreement on Investment (1998). The "Battle in Seattle" (1999) was followed up by similar clashes in Nice (2000), Genoa (2001), and Florence (2002). The Zapatista uprising of January 1, 1994, gave birth to a new cycle in Latin America, linking Hugo Chávez, Evo Morales, Lucio Guttiérez, the Argentinian popular uprisings of 2001–2, and Lula's 2002 victory in Brazil. Bensaïd renewed his regular trips to the continent. He was in Porto Alegre for the World Social Forums in 2002 and 2003.

The most transformative event of Bensaïd's personal life during these later years was his battle against AIDS. He contracted the syndrome in the mid-1990s during a trip to Brazil and, although managed by pharmaceuticals, it would deeply affect him for the rest of his life. Enzo Traverso has even argued that it had a major impact on the shape and pace of Bensaïd's thinking and writing:

"AIDS forbade him any long-term project; he worked frenetically because nothing could wait or be postponed." As a result, the books from the 1990s and early 2000s "remain the fragments of an extremely ambitious but unaccomplished work, prematurely interrupted. That was the ransom of an announced death."[48] This was perhaps the acceleration of a lifelong tendency. Bensaïd tended to work on a cluster of related works all at the same time, often approaching a set of connected themes from diverse angles. His was a "ceaselessly syncretic mind."[49] In the late 1980s and early 1990s, it was the role of the messianic and the theological, themes that figure prominently in *Moi, La Révolution* (1989), *Jeanne de Guerre lasse* (1991), and *Walter Benjamin, sentinelle messianique* (1990). He then turned to a sprawling three-volume study of Marx and Marxism. After being pushed by a publisher to edit this down dramatically, *Marx l'intempestif* and *La Discordance des temps* appeared simultaneously in autumn 1995. In the early 2000s, Bensaïd addressed more personal themes, not only in his autobiography *Une lente impatience* (2004), but also returning to the Jewish question in *Sur la question juive* (2006). Thus, in 2007, when Bensaïd published *The Dispossessed,* he was speaking from decades of struggle and self-transformation.

Daniel Bensaïd died in 2010 as a result of the cancerous effects of medication he had been taking to control AIDS. Returning to his work and continuing to renovate it for the present gives him new life. As he wrote in his autobiography, "As long as one claims that right to start again, the last word is never said."[50]

Notes on Translation

Daniel Bensaïd's essay was original published as *Les dépossédés: Karl* *Marx, les voleurs de bois et le droit des pauvres* (Paris: La fabrique, 2007). A modified French text was prepared for audiences in Quebec in 2008 by Lux Éditeur. German, Italian, Polish, and Spanish translations have also been published.

Bensaïd is a relatively clear and accessible writer, yet there are still challenges in translating his work. In this case, two persistent issues are pertinent. The title of the essay refers to *le droit des pauvres,* a phrasing repeated throughout the text. *Le droit* can mean both "law" and "right," depending on the context. Here it is most often used in the latter sense. In English it is awkward to speak of the "right of the poor" in the singular. Instead, English tends to refer to "rights" in the plural, which can more easily denote the subjective and possessive (i.e., *my* rights versus *yours*). This ambiguity is also evident in translations from German. In the Rhineland articles, for instance, Marx speaks of *Das Recht,* which carries precisely the same issues for English translation. These ambiguities of meaning have been deliberately preserved in the title of this book. A second issue concerns the word *la possession,* which is used frequently throughout. Depending on the context, this can be translated as either possession or ownership, because there is not the same linguistic distinction as in English. When Bensaid is speaking about the status or fact of having something, I have translated this as "possession." When he refers to the claim of legitimate title, I render it as "ownership."

In both the Bensaïd and Marx writings, a few rather technical legal terms have no direct literal translation in English because of differences in the historical development of the respective legal contexts. For instance, Bensaïd discusses *les ayants-droit,* which refers to rights holders who gain their claim on the basis of long-standing use or personal connection, which may be variously translated as "beneficiary," "entitlement claimant," and so on. It has been translated here as holders of "entitlement rights." In a similar vein, *Le droit d'aînesse* has been translated as "birthright." Marx occasionally mentions *der Ritterschaft,* which has been rendered as "knightly estate."

The appendix to Daniel Bensaïd's original *Les dépossédés* contained a heavily edited and abridged set of Marx's Rhineland articles. They have been restored here to their original full-length versions. Originals of Marx's articles on the Rhineland Parliament are published in the *Marx–Engels Gesamtausgabe* (Berlin: Gruyter, 1975–), Erste Abteilung, I/8. A previous English translation is available in *Marx and Engels Collected Works,* volume 1 (Chadwell Heath: Lawrence & Wishart, 2010), 224–63. These were originally translated by Clemens Palme Dutt, the early twentieth-century British–Indian Communist writer and translator. I benefited from this translation but have attempted to modernize it by updating the vocabulary and reorganizing the paragraphs into a more standard contemporary English format.

THE DISPOSSESSED

Karl Marx's Debates on Wood Theft and the Right of the Poor

Marx's articles on the "Debates on the Law concerning the Theft of Wood" were published in several editions of the *Rheinische Zeitung* between October 15 and November 3, 1842. Rhineland's civil society had inherited from the French Revolution and the Napoleonic occupation a juridical reform centered on the free disposal of private property and the abstract equality of legal subjects, breaking with the feudal traditions of Germanic law. A modern civil society had thus begun to emerge in conflict with the Prussian state. While the intellectuals of the petty bourgeoisie were rather attracted to French political life, the diffuse protest movements most committed to the defense of these freedoms against the restoration of the old order remained under the hegemony of the industrial and commercial bourgeoisie oriented toward England. Regardless of these internal differences, the liberal bourgeoisie of the Rhineland generally defended achievements of the revolution such as the maintenance of French juridical codes, municipal reform, and public liberties. In this way, they appeared out of step with the rest of the Prussian empire.

For thirty-five years the government in Berlin worked to suppress the liberalization of the region through a variety of oblique attacks and partial reforms, accompanied by an expansion of the Prussian administrative bureaucracy to ensure their local application. Measures aimed at the censorship of the press, which would lead to the closure of the *Rheinische Zeitung* in the spring of 1843, and to Marx's eventual voluntary exile in France, were part of this reactionary offensive. Until 1848, the issue of the Rhineland laws remained a standoff between the liberalism of the local region and the conservatism of the Prussian monarchy.

The region could not escape, however, the process of the gradual bureaucratic normalization begun in 1815. On March 16, 1821, French law was officially repealed and replaced by the law in force in the rest of the kingdom. In 1824, an order of the cabinet required the introduction of Prussian law into criminal proceedings. That same year, corporal punishment was reinstated in the prison system. In 1826, a new order satisfied the nobility by reestablishing birthright, thereby putting into question the principle of civil equality. To escape this reactionary movement, Heinrich Heine preceded Marx in 1831 on the road to exile in Paris.

I.

THE LAW ON THE THEFT OF WOOD AND THE RIGHT OF THE POOR

In this extended showdown between Rhineland liberalism and Prussian autocracy, the *Rheinische Zeitung* played the role of civil society's "proto-party." In 1842, Marx became the editor in chief. His correspondence with Bruno Bauer in 1841–42 reveals the importance he placed on the press as a vehicle for the practical realization of the theory advanced by their philosophical movement. In an article dated May 12, 1842, Marx juxtaposed the preventive censorship law, which "had only the *form* of law," to the "law of the press." Marx contended that only the latter was "real law because, in it, one found the positive existence of freedom."[1] In his article from January 1843, he reemphasized the close relationship between the press and the spirit of the people in forming public opinion and a public sphere. On January 21, the Prussian censors decided that the *Rheinische Zeitung* would no longer be published, effective April 1.

In articles from January 13 supporting the work of Moselle correspondents on the situation of the Rhineland winemakers, Marx reiterated that "the newspaper correspondent, by transmitting conscientiously the voice of the people as it comes to his ears," can only "consider himself a minor part of a complex organism, in which he freely chooses a function."[2] Following this logic, Marx claimed the right of anonymity "due to the nature of the daily press." (His articles were not signed and, well after his death, Engels was still hesitant to authenticate them.) Proper names "would rigidly isolate each article, just as the body isolates us from one another." It would "totally negate the fact that each article was only a complementary member," and that the newspaper is "the place where numerous individual opinions are gathered" in order to form a "single mind." There is no better way to express the partisan function assigned to the *Rheinische Zeitung*.

Four days later, Marx went back on the offensive: "Produced by public opinion, the free press also produces public opinion." The free press, he argued, acts not only as "the people's mind, but also as an expression of its heart."[3] This insistence on the function of public debate clearly conforms to the liberal tradition of the Enlightenment, defined as it is by the public exercise of critical reason. In the Rhineland of the 1830s, the tension between civil society and the state was at the heart of public controversy. The censorship regulations of December 24, 1841 (not published until January 14, 1842), arrived as a major event in this context. Marx immediately responded: "A law that attacks these principles is not state law made for citizens, but rather a law made by one faction against another." It is not, therefore, a law properly speaking, but only a "privilege": "A society where one component believes itself to be the unique and exclusive bearer of *raison d'État* and of the concrete morality of the state, where the government opposes itself in principle to the people," is a society where "bad conscience invents laws of revenge."

In 1859, looking back on "the development of his own studies in political economy," Marx recalled this context of conflict in which he had been led to focus directly on social issues: "In 1842–43, I was forced, in my capacity as editor-in-chief of the *Rheinische Zeitung,* to speak for the first time, *and with great embarrassment,* about so-called material interests. Debates in the Rhineland parliament on the theft of wood and the portioning of landed property; the polemic launched by Herr von Schaper, then

Oberpräsident of the Rhine Province, against the Gazette about the situation of the Moselle farmers; and finally the debates on free trade and protectionism gave me the opportunity to concern myself with economic issues for the first time."[4] It was in the midst of this full-on fight for the survival of the newspaper that Marx made the fateful decision late in 1842 to break with the Berlin faction of the neo-Hegelian movement. This break was a first step in his evolution from Rhineland liberalism to socialism. This rupture took place at the same time as the series of articles on the theft of wood, announced in the Kreuznach manuscripts during the summer of 1843, in which Marx settles his accounts with the legacy of Hegel's philosophy of the state. It also generated two major articles, the *Introduction to the Critique of Hegel's Philosophy of Right* and *On the Jewish Question,* published in Paris at the beginning of 1844 in a stand-alone issue of *Deutsch-Französische Jahrbücher.* In these texts (in which the proletariat makes its dramatic entrance to his work), Marx denounced the "political illusion" of taking civic emancipation as the last word in "human emancipation" and placed on the agenda a new, unprecedented, unheard-of *social revolution.*[5]

"Rural Pauperism" and "Forest Malfeasance"

As a turning point, 1842–43 marks the overcoming of what Louis Althusser has called Marx's "liberal rationalist moment." In the shedding of this earlier moment, the controversy over the "theft of wood" figures prominently. It was a response to the Rhineland parliament's June 1842 deliberations over a "Report on the Theft of Timber and other Forest Products" *[Bericht zum Diebstahl von Holz und anderer Forstprodukte].* This report is part of a series of measures, including the Forest Act of July 1841, which was completed in 1843 by the introduction of a new system of hunting. The legislative powers and privileges of the provincial assemblies were severely curtailed by Berlin's central power. The Rhineland parliament was composed of deputies from the various "estates" (from the city, the countryside, and the nobility), each of which had an equal number of votes (twenty-five for each of the three, which amounts to overrepresentation of the nobility). Land rent and public tax contributions were the only eligibility criteria taken into consideration for representatives from both the cities and the countryside.

The bill submitted to the parliament on behalf of Friedrich-Wilhelm, "King of Prussia by the grace of God," concerns the "following threatened goods" *[dérobements]*: "(1) All timber not yet felled; (2) All green wood outside the forest destined for use; (3) All fallen wood, or toppled trunks not yet cut up; (4) Chips and lumber lying in the forest or wood deposits not yet gathered up." The different articles established rules for evaluating offenses and their corresponding penalties, according to whether "the theft was committed during the night or on a holiday"; if "the offender was concealed or had blackened his face" in order to avoid being recognized; if he gave false information about his identity, etc. Article 14 further stipulates that "All fines due to the theft of wood are owed directly to the forest owners, even if paid for by various accomplices and beneficiaries, just as is all forced labor in cases of insolvent convicts." Article 16 specifies: "If a fine cannot be recovered because of the poverty of the offender or any persons responsible in his place, it will be replaced by labor or imprisonment." And Article 19 adds: "The forced labor of the offender shall consist in forestry work for the owner of the forest."

The series of articles Marx composed concerning the debates on the theft of wood, published between October 25 and November 3, are part of a collection devoted to debates in the Rhineland parliament. Along with later writings on the situation of the Moselle peasants, these are the only pieces to address the social question directly. In 1851, the future mayor of Cologne, Hermann Becker, reissued those of Marx's articles that had originally been published between 1842 and 1851. This is why relevant sections of the *Rheinische Zeitung*, including articles on the theft of wood, corrected by hand for this reissue, could be found much later in the municipal archives of Cologne.

The emergence of wood theft, to which the parliament's bill is responding, clearly appears as a consequence of rural pauperism in full bloom.[6] It is a question of punishing the illegal appropriation of timber and other forest products by a massively impoverished peasantry, so much so that this appropriation no longer simply targets the immediate consumption of wood, but also its sale as a commodity (at this time firewood is a highly sought-after raw material). Pierre Lascoumes and Hartwig Zander cite the following list of "forest infractions and their economic causes" established by forest rangers: theft of blueberries and other berries; theft of forest products necessary for the production of brushes and brooms, or as food for livestock; theft of twigs for the production of fishing rods; theft of timber for the repair of domestic and agricultural implements; theft of wood for roof shingles; theft of timber for hop-poles; theft of wood for stairs, trestles, and scaffolding; theft of ground roots for basket weaving; theft of fagots for firewood . . . an edifying inventory! It is composed of all those marketable goods without which life itself could not be secured, especially as their domestic use was itself increasingly subject to market circulation.

Lascoumes and Zander summarize well the substance of the dispute: "The Prussian State was required to settle once and for all legal issues relating to the contradiction between rights of entitlement and rights of ownership.[7] This question led to the problem of individual enjoyment of property acquired by usufruct. Could wood distributed on the basis of entitlement be considered the property of these claimants, or should it be classified as a 'natural good' that is only to be used for the immediate satisfaction of basic needs? We can understand the importance of this issue if we recall that the national tax policy could in no case admit that mere entitlement claimants act as full owners, lest they appear as competitors in a monopolized market that national policy manages according to the principle of sale to the highest bidder."[8] The dilemma derives from the fact that the integration of timber into an exchange market rendered its use-value and exchange-value inseparable from one another. At stake in the new legislation was the need to assert property rights, rigorously distinguishing property titles from entitlements based on need, and thus the exchange economy from the subsistence economy. The evolution of an apparatus of penal sanctions thereby institutionalized new forms of delinquency and social criminality.

In bringing the issue of the partition of landed property "down to earth," Marx readily admits to not having access to the bill itself, but only to the parliament's "draft amendments" and an incomplete account of its proceedings. At issue in the debate is the very definition of property. The bill also intended to include the uprooting of "green trees" as well as the collecting of dead twigs as instances of theft. In both cases, such "appropriation of foreign timber" would qualify as misdemeanor "theft": "To appropriate green wood," Marx sarcastically comments, "it must be violently extracted from the organic whole to which it belongs. If this is clearly an attack on the integrity of the tree, it is just as manifestly an attack on the rights of the tree owner. Moreover, if cut wood is stolen from a third party, this timber is the product of the owner. Timber is already transformed. The natural connection to property replaces the artificial one. Therefore, whomsoever steals timber steals property. By contrast, the gathering of twigs does not disturb property. One is disturbing property that has already been disturbed. The thief carries his own authority to cast judgment against property. The gathering of twigs is merely to execute the judgment already rendered by nature itself: you only possess the tree, the tree no longer possesses the branches in question. The gathering of twigs and the theft of wood are therefore two essentially different things. The object is different, as is the action relating to the object, and the intention behind the act. And what other objective criteria should we apply to the intention if not the content and form of the action? And, ignoring this essential difference, you call both actions theft and punish them both accordingly."[9]

Marx thus challenges the logic of the law by pretending to view it from the point of view of the owner whose claimed property right would be legitimized by the fact that the tree grows on his estate, or that manufactured timber (transformed by labor) comes from it. He who gathers twigs would therefore be entitled to advance an argument arising from a legitimate interpretation of a supposedly natural right: dead wood no longer belongs to the tree, nor, consequently, to the owner of the tree. It follows that the two acts cannot be united under one and the same offense, except by ignoring the different intentions behind them. Marx mischievously suggests that such a conflation could just as well turn against the owner. This "brutal point of view," which "recognizes only a common disposition behind different actions and therefore abstracts from any differentiation," would end up negating itself: "By regarding all attacks on property as instances of theft without distinction or further determination, would not all private property be theft?" The controversy then moves from the question of the delimitation of a legitimate right of property to that of the legitimacy of private property as such, raised two years earlier by Proudhon in his study *What Is Property?*

The second angle of attack against the bill deals with the problematic relation between crime and punishment: "In property crime, the importance of the value of the property in determining the penalty goes without saying. Just as the concept of crime requires punishment, the reality of crime requires a measurement of penalty. Actual crime is limited. In order to be effective, the penalty must likewise be limited. To be just, the penalty must be based on a principle of law. Since the objective is to do harm to the real consequences of crime, the penalty should appear to the offender as the necessary effect of *his own actions*. The limit of the penalty should be set by his own action. The specific *content* by which he is infringed upon is the limit of the specified crime. The measure of the content of the penalty is therefore the measure of the crime. This measure of the property is its value. If personhood is always a totality whatever its limits, property exists only in a limit which is not only determinable but determined, not only measurable but measured. Value is the existence of property in civil society, the logical conclusion by which the existence of the property acquires its intelligibility and social communicability."[10]

Judicial quantification is presented as a system of equivalence and proportion between crime and punishment. In an attack against property, the extent of the penalty expresses the "intelligible and communicable" social measure of property. By entrusting a forest ranger, who is "in the service of the forest owner and paid by him," with the assessment of damages, by guaranteeing "the job security of the informing guard," and in condemning the defendant to a fine or to forced labor payable directly to the owner, the bill is unable to "rise to the standpoint of the state." On the contrary, it puts the "medium of private property into contradiction with reason and law." This logic turns "the employee of the forest owners into a public authority," and likewise transforms public authorities into employees of the forest landlords. This confusion of public and private, of seigniorial gendarme with civil courts, perpetuates "seigniorial jurisdiction" to the detriment of the state and of rational law.

Hybrid and Uncertain Property

The modern distinction between private and public, and its application to property rights, is what lies behind the parliamentary debates over the theft of wood. As evidenced by the judicial statistics of the time, the quantitative importance of timber theft illustrates both the vigor of customary practices of usufruct rights and the growing criminalization of such practices by an emergent capitalist society. This period of transition represents a decisive moment in the redefinition of property relations. As historian E. P. Thompson noted in the context of eighteenth-century England, law becomes a primary means by which to impose "new definitions of property" for the benefit of owners "by eradicating undefined rights of land use, or accelerating the enclosure movement."[11] The suppression of any entanglement of personal and collective rights exerted on the same property manifested an opposition between two antagonistic conceptions of property, which would be resolved in favor of the right of absolute private ownership: "the importance of litigation in matters of forestry management attests therefore, on the one hand, to the establishment of a new property code and, more broadly, to the imposition of a legal system based on individualism (the condition of generalized exchange) breaking with customary principles."[12]

This is exactly what Marx notes in his article when he recalls how the closure of convents and subsequent removal of their aid to the poor deprived the needy of an "ancient right"—without compensation—thereby pushing them out to get skinned on the job market. This arose in part because "all customary rights of the poor were based on the fact that certain kinds of property had *an indeterminate character* that undermined any final decision of whether the property was ultimately private or communal." The brutal suppression of these "hybrid and uncertain property forms" involves the simultaneous withdrawal of obligations toward the poor derived from this "undecided property" and its public privileges. However, the new, modern, rational understanding of law had to ignore the fact that, "from the point of view of strictly private law," it was then faced with a dual system of law, that of the "haves" and the "have-nots." Preoccupied with giving property a civil character and protecting the rights of owners, the new law fails to recognize that "some objects of property cannot by their nature ever acquire a determinant private property form and thus fall to the right of occupancy by their very essence and continent existence; these objects belong therefore to occupancy rights of that class of people who, excluded by law from all other property forms, occupies in civil society the same position as objects in nature." In other words, the new law claimed to abolish the inalienable right of the poor to common property offered by nature.

The invocation of a "natural status" to these objects seems to refer to the tradition of natural law in which the invocation of "occupancy rights," or *jus nullius,* accords a right of first occupancy onto a "personal good." It is this juridical rationale that was used to legalize the colonial appropriation of lands decreed "virgin." Marx exploits the paradoxical logic of the argument: if property is not legitimated by an activity that transforms the object (through mixing with labor, as it is with Locke), then the right of occupation derives from an initial stroke of force (a "seizure of the land" in the case of colonial conquests). Such a right is universalizable. It must also benefit that class of people who, "excluded from all property," find themselves in a sort of pre-civil and pre-juridical state of nature (much like the objects in question). These formulations anticipate the more elaborate ones that we find the following year in the *Introduction to the Critique of Hegel's Philosophy of Right*. The possibility of German emancipation lies "in the formation of a class with radical chains, a class of bourgeois civil society that is not a class of bourgeois civil society, an estate the dissolution of which would be the dissolution of all social estates." This class then receives its proper name: "The particular class through which society itself will be dissolved is the proletariat."

Market versus Popular Economy

Was Marx content to oppose the old customary rights to the contractual formalism of juridical right, or does this merely serve to expose the contradictions in which the new legislation is entangled? Undoubtedly, the second. This is to highlight the inconsistencies resulting from the tension between a civil society based on the generalization of contractual relations, on the one hand, and a state that is supposedly representative of a noncontractual general interest. These contradictions mark the limits of the "merely political" emancipation analyzed the following year in "On the Jewish Question."[13] The reference to customary law here is not, however, a mere discursive tactic. Under the influence of the French Revolution, taxation rights had to give ground to the peasantry through the recognition of ancient usufruct in state forests. The indeterminacy of a certain property type, hybrid or indecisive, straddling private and communal property, corresponded to feudal forms of socialized land use. The right to the commons mainly dealt with matters of livestock (right-of-way, grazing, gleaning) and forestry (collection of timber). From the seventeenth century, new nobles set about to trim these collective rights. In France, the *Grande Ordonnance de Colbert sur les Eaux et Forêts* [Colbert Ordinance on Waters and Forests] in August 1669 restricted the right of gleaning to four months of the year and prohibited the grazing of sheep and the collecting of dead wood. These restrictions led to well-documented peasant resistance movements.

Whenever man, taken as an individual subject and partner to a contract, becomes the general measure of social practices, property comes to be defined in relation to him as private property. In the classical age, property steadily evolved toward an "absolutist" form. Property went from being a "gift of nature" to a "basic right,"[14] from a condition of plenty to a subjective right: "the absolutism of property primarily entailed the abolition of the relativity of feudal property, in which one could be simultaneously the property holder relative to one person and yet indebted to another with respect to the same land."[15] Subjective right is not restricted to the regulation of interindividual relations; it also authorizes juridical action. Carrier of a dynamic expansion of its field of application, the modern notion of property thereby entered into conflict with the old conception, which had been largely based on passive possession. Thus, the enclosure movement (the appropriation of communal lands by large landowners) begun in England in the late fifteenth century received its legal anointing in the eighteenth. Consequently, "the law itself became an instrument of plunder."[16]

This assessment did not occur without violent social conflicts. Karl Polanyi has drawn attention to "the great fact of social solidarity" that for forty years delayed the establishment of a competitive labor market in England. This fact now goes by the name Speenhamland, the Berkenshire locale where the nobility decided in 1795 to give a living wage to the poor of each parish, indexed to the price of bread and basic rents, regardless of whether they worked or not. It was not until 1834 that this system (which had been expanded in the intervening years) was replaced by a new poor law. Recognizing a "right to live," Polanyi notes that "until abolished in 1834, [the Speenhamland law] effectively prevented the establishment of a competitive labour market."[17]

The Poor Law of 1834 signified therefore the abolition of the "right to live":

> The scientific cruelty of that Act was so shocking to public sentiment in the 1830s and 1840s that the vehement contemporary protests blurred the picture in the eyes of posterity. Many of the most needy poor, it was true, were left to their fate as outdoor relief was withdrawn, and among those who suffered most bitterly were the "deserving poor" who were too proud to enter the workhouse which had become an abode of shame. Never perhaps in all modern history has a more ruthless act of social reform been perpetrated; it crushed multitudes of lives while merely pretending to provide a criterion of genuine destitution in the workhouse test . . . Yet the bulk of the complaints were really due to the abruptness with which an institution of old standing was uprooted and a radical transformation rushed into effect . . . However, if money incomes alone had counted, the condition of the people would soon have been deemed improved . . . If Speenhamland had prevented the emergence of a working class, now the laboring poor were being formed into such a class by the pressure of an unfeeling mechanism. If under Speenhamland the people had been taken care of as none too precious beasts deserved to be, now they were expected to take care of themselves, with all the odds against them. If Speenhamland meant the snug misery of degradation, now the laboring man was homeless in society. If Speenhamland had overworked the values of neighborhood, family, and rural surroundings, now man was detached from home and kin, torn from his roots and all meaningful environment. In short, if Speenhamland meant the rot of immobility, now the peril was that of death through exposure.[18]

For Polyani, it is clear that evaluating the social conditions of the poor depends entirely on whether this is measured in terms of monetary solubility or guaranteed basic needs. Marx made a similar remark when, in the 1844 *Introduction to the Critique of the Philosophy of Right,* he distinguished poverty resulting from natural conditions (natural disasters, environmental vagaries) from "artificially produced poverty" generated by modern social relations of exploitation.

—

The initiators of the Speenhamland law were certainly not pure philanthropists. They undoubtedly sought to maintain the status quo in social and family relationships, and to cushion the devastating effects of the primitive accumulation of capital. Their vision of the world included a mixture of religious considerations and traditions. This is what the historian E. P. Thompson defines in the context of the European famine riots as a "moral" or "popular economy"—that is, an "economy subject to the natural right to existence"—a right that would inspire the subordination of property to the right to existence [le droit d'exister] in the French Constitution of Year II (1793).

According to Thompson, almost all popular movements of the eighteenth century reveal a sense of legitimacy based on defending traditional customs and rights. Upon drafting his Declaration of the Rights of Man on August 23, 1789, Marat was one of the few to explain the antagonism between property right and the right to existence [le droit d'exister]: "As long as nature offers ample food and clothing to mankind, all will be well and peace will reign on Earth. But he who lacks everything has the right to snatch the excesses that abound for another . . . To save his own life, man is entitled to assault property, liberty, indeed the very life of his fellow man."[19] On December 2, 1789, Robespierre, denouncing the combined evils of economic liberalism and martial law, became the most scrupulous defender of property, openly declaring that by this term he meant "the right to rob and murder his fellow man":

> How, then, can one pretend that every kind of restriction or regulation on the sale of wheat is an attack on property, and disguise this barbarous system under the specious name of free trade?[20]

Putting the revolutionary movement to the test, Robespierre eventually concluded that the first of all inalienable rights is the right to existence: "In defining liberty as the highest good and most sacred of rights obtained from nature, you rightly say that it functions as a limit on other rights. Why don't you apply this to the social institution of property? It is as if the eternal laws of nature were less inviolable than human conventions."[21] During the winter of Year II, class struggle in France drove the conflict between property rights and the rights to existence to a breaking point.[22] It is in the name of this "popular political economy" that Robespierre responded in his speech of May 10, 1793, to the arguments of the liberal economists.

Florence Gauthier and Guy-Robert Ikni see in this "popular political economy" the expression of "a political liberalism of universal natural right in which the right to liberty is inextricably linked to the right to life and livelihood."[23] They conclude that a contradiction arose between "political liberty and economic freedom, that is to say, a contradiction within natural law, between the particular right of ownership over material goods, and the universal right to life and liberty, leading the ownership class [les propriétaires] to abandon the humanism of the Enlightenment and reject universal natural law."[24] Half a century later, in the shadow of the barricades of June 1848, the challenge of this social war between property forms was no longer in any doubt: "Soon there will be a great political struggle between the 'haves' and the 'have nots'; property will be its battlefield and all major political questions will turn on the extent of the transformation to the rights of owners."[25] Tocqueville's contemporary heirs take after him.

In his 1842 articles, Marx draws upon customary right to critique the firming up of the right of private appropriation and the restrictions on popular rights that are its necessary corollary. Of course, Marx is undoubtedly aware of the ambiguities of custom and tradition. He knows all too well that custom is a vast category, capable of covering a variety of diverse and opposing interests. Thus "so-called customary privileges" are only "customs contrary to law," whose origins go back to a time when human history was only a part of natural history. Feudalism is again the "reign of the animal over the spiritual," and customary privileges are the expression of an animal inequality fixed in law: "When the privileged call for a legal right to their customary claims, they demand an animal, rather than properly human, form for law. They turn law into an animal mask."

Marx will have nothing to do with nostalgia for the "use and customs" of yesteryear. On the contrary, in an article from August 12, 1842, he dismisses the "philosophical manifesto of the school of historical right" as "the German theory of the *Ancien Régime*." He seeks only to identify the social significance attached to the theft of wood, that is, the constitutional delegitimation of custom as a competing source of law. Similarly, it is against this state monopolization of the production of law that the German Historical School of Hugo, Grimm, Savigny, and Beseler also protested, on behalf of a continuity of customary regulations rooted in specific national history. But they did so from the standpoint of feudal privilege, not from the perspective of the customary rights of the poor.

Marx's approach is entirely distinct. His aim was to flush out the conflict between two antagonistic forms of right from behind customary ecumenism: "If the customary rights of the nobility are contrary to the very idea of rational law, the customary rights of the poor are contrary to the tradition of positive law." It is the customary rights of the *poor,* not those of the privileged, that attack this "enlightened legislation." Through customary right, the poor instinctually knew how to seize indeterminate forms of property to satisfy their natural needs. They considered the "alms of nature" to be their rightful property: "In gathering, this most basic class of human society confronts the products of the elemental power of nature and puts them in order. This is also the case for wild products acquired by a pure accident of possession; in virtue of their insignificance they are not the labor products of any true owner. This is also the case for gleaning, that second harvest, and other customary rights of this sort." Often regarded as a natural source of law, custom is itself a contradictory social construction. All talk of "popular customs" as a means of opposing feudal privileges is therefore mere tautology. Customary law is itself an expression of power relations.

In this sense, we can juxtapose the "customary rights of the poor" to the formal equality found between parties in the contract. In the latter, a fool's contract is sanctified in the name of "human rights" whose proclaimed universality covers the particular interests of the ruling class:

> We unpractical people, however, demand for the poor, politically and socially dispossessed [non possédante] multitude what the learned and teachable servility of so-called historians has discovered to be the true philosopher's stone for turning every unfair presumption into the pure gold of right. We demand for the poor a *customary right,* and indeed not one that is only of a local character but is a customary right of the poor in all countries. We go still further and maintain that a customary right by its very nature can *only* be a right of this lowest, dispossessed and elemental mass.[26]

"Between equal rights," Marx wrote in *Capital,* "force decides." Force likewise determines between conflicting customary rights. Accordingly, one can follow through social history the red thread that connects ancient customary right (the "moral economy" of the poor) to the rights to life, existence, employment, income, housing, all opposed to the rights of private property.

II.

A SOCIAL WAR OF PROPERTIES

During the English Revolution of 1649, the Levellers considered individual property-in-the-person to be the foundation of constitutions, and not vice versa.[27] In his *Appeal* of July 1647, the Leveller Overton proclaims: "To each person living on earth is naturally given an individual right of property that no one has the right to violate or usurp, for what makes me what I am is that I am owner of myself. Without possession of myself, I would not be me. No one has power over my rights and liberties; and I have no power over the rights and liberties of others." To be free is to own oneself and, by extension, the means and the products of one's labor.[28] The Levellers' point of departure is not, therefore, a critique of property, but rather a conception of equality buttressed by a theological argument. At the meeting of October 1647 in Putney, under the chairmanship of Cromwell and his son-in-law [Henry] Ireton, the main controversy turned on the decision over whether to restrict voting rights to the propertied. The Leveller Sexby was indignant: "There are many thousands of us soldiers that have ventured our lives; we have had little propriety in the kingdom as our estates, yet we have had a birthright. But it seems now, except as a man hath a fixed estate in this kingdom, he hath no right . . . I wonder we were so much deceived."[29]

Another Leveller, Rainsborough, adds: “I see that it is impossible to have liberty but all property must be taken away. If it be laid down for a rule, and if you will say it, it must be so. But I would fain know what the solider hath fought for all this while? He hath fought to enslave himself, to give power to men of riches, men of estates, to make him a perpetual slave. We do find in all presses that go forth none must be pressed that are freehold men.”[30] The critique of property derives from the defense of freedom and equality, leading to a distinction between property in the person and “property as a form of goods.”

In 1649, the radicalization of the revolutionary process led to a new core issue: what the Levellers would do regarding the ancient right of the poor and the restoration of communal lands for the benefit of the poor. The indictment of the “*unmasked Tyranipocrite,*” dated August 14, directly involves the collusion of power and property: “The powerful shall be mightily punished, for the sins of the rulers are multiple and unacceptable: do you not steal, you who command others not to steal? Do you not remain idle, you who order others to work? Are you not proud, you who would teach others humility? These rich and clever thieves do not operate along the roads to seize our purses, nor sneak through our windows. They have found a more cunning and unholy way to steal than even we poor fools. They think they are safe, since the law and the executioner serve them and dare not hang them. Since they are thieves by Act of Parliament, they are not thieves at all! Indeed, all they steal and rob is their own, according to the law of the jungle. If necessary, they can even present you with all the parchments stating that such and such country, city, town, village, land, or house ultimately belongs to them anyway.” In his address the same year in the House of Commons, Peter Chamberlen claimed the following for England’s poor: “(1) What remains of the lands, goods and tenures; (2) All that is owed on the public accounts; (3) All that is actually due to the poor in wild lands, forests, heaths, moors, hunting lands . . . (4) And all mines not being exploited, any flooded land or captured from the sea.”[31]

In response to this great revolutionary shock, Hobbes sought to shield private property from its detractors in the name of an egalitarian natural right, a secularized form of the equality of creatures before God. For Hobbes, property is an institution founded and guaranteed by the state:

> Seventhly, is annexed to the sovereignty, the whole power of prescribing the rules, whereby every man may know, what goods he may enjoy, and what actions he may do, without being molested by any of his fellow-subjects: and this is it men call *propriety* . . . The distribution of the materials of this nourishment, is the constitution of *mine,* and *thine,* and *his;* that is to say, in one word *propriety*; and belongeth in all kinds of commonwealth to the sovereign power. For where there is no commonwealth, there is (as hath been already shown) a perpetual war of every man against his neighbour; and therefore every thing is his that getteth it, and keepeth it by force; which is neither *propriety,* nor *community*; but *uncertainty* . . . A fifth doctrine, that tendeth to the dissolution of a commonwealth, is, *that every private man has an absolute propriety in his goods; such, as excludeth the right of the sovereign.* Every man has indeed a propriety that excludes the right of every other subject: and he has it only from the sovereign power; without the protection whereof, every other man should have equal rights to the same.[32]

All the same, Hegel will later affirm in the *Principles of the Philosophy of Right* the primacy of the "right of necessity" [le droit de détresse] over the right of property:

> In extreme danger and in collision with the rightful property of someone else, this life may claim (not in equity, but as a right) a right of necessity; for the alternatives are an infinite injury [Verletzung] to existence with total loss of rights, and an injury only to an individual and limited existence of freedom . . . From the right of necessity arises the benefit of competence, whereby a debtor is permitted

> to retain his tools, agricultural implements, clothes, and in general as much of his resources—i.e. of the property of his creditors—as is deemed necessary to support him, even in his accustomed station in society . . . Such necessity [Not] reveals the finitude and hence the contingency of both right and welfare—of the abstract existence [Dasein] of freedom as distinct from the existence [Existenz] of the particular person, and of the sphere of the particular will as distinct from the universality of right.[33]

This right of necessity is therefore not a "gracious concession," a public and compassionate form of charity, but rather an enforceable right to property in situations of social urgency.

In his support of the Moselle correspondent for the *Rheinische Zeitung* over against von Schaper, the president of the provincial assembly, Marx also uses the term "necessity" [détresse]. In the article of January 15, 1843, he defends the rough style of those who "perceive immediately and frequently the pitiless voice of indigence wherever the people are found." This is where "political duty" publicly takes up the "popular language of necessity [détresse]."

The Right of Necessity versus the Right of Property

In Marx's articles on the theft of wood and on the situation of the Moselle wine growers, the question of property reveals above all the contradictions at work in the relationship between civil society and the state. Marx addresses these contradictions from a liberal-rationalist point of view, however. In Hegelian fashion, he highlights the fact that the inconsistencies of the modern state stand behind the question of law, inconsistencies that undermine its claim to universal rationality: "If it becomes clear here that private interests have reduced the state to a mere medium of private interest, does it not follow that the representatives of private interests (the social estates or *Stände*) want and need to cut back the state in the name of that interest? Every modern state that conforms so poorly to its very concept will be forced by the first practical test of its legislative power to exclaim: 'Your ways are not mine and your ideas are not mine!'"

This practical refutation of the claims of the modern state is revealed to be true through the inversion of its supposed relation with civil society. Far from embodying the public interest through legislation, such as concerns the theft of wood, public authorities put themselves at the behest of private interests. By reducing itself to the aggregative sum of the contractual relations woven into civil society, the state contradicts the superior rationality attributed to it by Hegel: "But the state is by no means a contract, and its substantial essence does not consist unconditionally in the production and safeguarding of the lives and property of individuals as such. The state is rather that higher instance which may even lay claim to the lives and property of individuals and require their sacrifice."[34] This reduction of the state to a sum of private contractual relations is manifestly revealed for Marx by the system of sanctions imposed by the law on "culprits" of forest crimes. By requiring the payment of fines directly to the owner or, failing that, the carrying out of forced labor in his service, a public penalty is transformed into private compensation: "Could the forest owner get better insurance for his wood than he does here, whereby crime was converted into an annuity? A clever general, he converts an attack upon him into an infallible opportunity for spoils of war." In the exercise of its sovereign function, the state then behaves as common insurer of the owners. "*Punishment* as such, the restoration of the law, which must certainly be distinguished from restitution of the value and compensation for loss, the restoration of private property, is transformed from *a public punishment* into *a private compensation,* the fines going not to the state treasury, but to the private coffers of the forest owner . . . The wood possesses the remarkable character such that as soon as it is stolen it secures for its owner state qualities it did not previously possess . . . The wood thief has robbed the forest owner of wood, but the forest owner has used the wood thief to steal the *state itself.*"[35]

The case of wood theft thus provided Marx with the opportunity to draw general conclusions about the reality of the state and its functions vis-à-vis civil society. The Rhineland parliament had not failed in its mission of embodying the general interest. On the contrary, it "fulfilled its mission perfectly": "Conforming to its vocation, the assembly represented a particular, determinate interest and treated this as its final end. That it trampled upon the law was simply the consequence of its duty, because interest is, by its nature, a blind instinct, without limits, partial, in a word, beyond the law." Even if he declared that he followed these "insipid and bland debates" only "with repugnance," Marx still did not regret the time he devoted to them. The challenge was worth it. The aim was to discover and show by example that "what one could expect from a meeting of the estates *(Stände),* an assembly of special interests, if it was called upon to legislate seriously." Contra this type of corporate meeting, Marx mounted a passionate defense of universal suffrage, at the risk of underestimating the fact that such suffrage can also achieve, in more devious and less visible ways, "an assembly of special interests."

In good liberal-rationalist manner, when faced with the mystification of a state founded upon a false universality and rationality, Marx assigns in his texts from 1842–43 a major role to civil society via freedom of the press and the constitution of a public sphere for the confrontation of opposing social interests. This theme will return later but will be transformed into the prospect of a "withering away of the state," not by its dissolution—or that of law itself—into "bourgeois civil society," or by the disappearance of the political into the administration of things, but by the effective supersession of the great modern split between civil society and the state, economics and politics, private and public, the rights of man and the rights of citizen, political revolution and social revolution.

"Property Is Theft!"

Prior to the major turning in Marx's political formation represented by the censorship of the *Rheinische Zeitung* and the 1844 *Annales Franco-allemandes* essays, the articles on the theft of wood constitute Marx's first foray into the controversies (then in full swing) over the definition and boundaries of property. Proudhon's 1840 text *What Is Property?* was one of the most famous polemics of the time, while Édouard Laboulaye's *A History of Property* had also just been honored by the Académie Française (1838).[36]

In the seventeenth century, with the English and Dutch revolutions, transformations in property and the emergence of a new balance between public and private had become a burning issue. The French Revolution constitutionally sacralized property, which, in the liberal revolutionary spirit, was considered the foundation and guarantee of the individual freedom of citizens. It was, however, immediately desecrated again by the fact of being opposed to a right of existence, especially via the establishment of price restrictions on bread and basic necessities imposed under the pressure of *la sans-culotterie* in the Year II.[37] By contrast, because its very legitimacy had become problematic, the Napoleonic Civil Code attached itself all the more to an expansive definition of property right, "a fundamental right on which all institutions are based." Section 544 of the code declared property the "right to enjoy and dispose of things in the most absolute way" under the law. It thereby produced constraints and limits on customary and familial rights through property law.

The debate rebounds all the more beautifully after the great bourgeois panic of June 1848. In September of that year, Thiers published his memoir, *On Property,* which defined private property as the foundation of an unlimited, exclusive, and absolute right, subject to the will of a person, and belonging to the proprietor "to the exclusion of all else."[38] The triumph of this Thermidorian conception of property was the revenge of the victors of June 1848 over the spirit of Rousseau, who had inspired the members of the National Convention *(les Conventionnels)* in the turmoil of 1793.[39] *The Discourse on the Origins of Inequality* thus haunts the revolution: "The first person who, having enclosed a plot of land, took it into his head to say *this is mine* and found people simple enough to believe him, was the true founder of civil society."[40] As a social institution, property has a history and its concept "does not form all in one stroke in the human mind." The perennial right of the producer to the means and the products of his labor had been "readily converted" into the simple ownership of property. This formed a new sort of right, a "property right differing from that arising in natural law." In historicizing the concept of property, Rousseau problematizes its legitimacy. His text conveyed the underlying supposition of the laws (as well as the imagined original social contract) as that which "gave new barriers to the weak and new powers to the rich, irrevocably destroyed natural liberty, and forever solidified the law of property and inequality." As such, it marked a true epochal shift.

Compared to the attempts to found the legitimacy of property upon a natural right of appropriation through occupation or labor, Rousseau's inversion is radical. Property rights are, for Rousseau, nothing but "a human convention and institution." Accordingly, although "every man can dispose of what he possesses as he sees fit . . . it is not the same for the essential gifts of nature such as life and liberty, which everyone is allowed to enjoy, and of which it is at least doubtful that one has the right to divest himself."[41] This positions the inalienable right to existence (to "life"!) against any right to private property.

The very meaning of the concept of property was thus transformed, gradually and in proportion to the extension of market relations, as capital penetrated into the sphere of production and separated the worker from the means of production. For early liberalism, this signaled the founding of individual autonomy and the transition from feudal subjection to modern citizenship. For rapidly maturing capitalism, this signaled the right to private appropriation of the means of production and the dispossession of the worker, not only from his land or his tools, but his own personhood, which he was then forced to sell at market. It is this contradiction, registered in the multiple meanings of the word *property* itself, which Proudhon laid bare in his 1840 essay, in which he sought to rebut the dual legitimation of private property by occupation and labor, by demonstrating that the first prevents property and the second destroys it. He defined the right of occupation as "a natural method of dividing the earth among labourers as fast as they appear." But if every man has a natural right to occupation of the earth simply because he exists, "it follows that the quantity of material which each labourer may claim varies with the number of occupants." Since the right of occupancy is "always subordinate to population," it can therefore "never remain fixed, and so it is impossible for it to ever become property." The right of occupancy is thus condemned to disappear "if it is in conflict with the public interest, which, being the social interest, is also that of the occupant."[42]

That's why jurists have abandoned the theoretical defense of the right of occupancy to focus instead on labor as that which gives rise to property. This legitimation of property through work is in effect at the heart of Locke's *Second Treatise of Government*:

> Though the earth, and all inferior creatures, be common to all men, yet every man has a property in his own person: this nobody has any right to but himself. The labour of his body, and the work of his hands, we may say, are properly his. Whatsoever then he removes out of the state that nature hath provided, and left it in, he hath mixed his labour with, and joined to it something that is his own, and thereby makes it his property. It being by him removed from the common state nature hath placed it in, it hath by this labour something annexed to it that excludes the common right of other men. For this labour being the unquestionable property of the labourer, no man but he can have a right to what that is once joined to, at least where there is enough, and as good, left in common for others.[43]

Proudhon basically replies that if labor is the foundation of property rights, then no one should be able to be dispossessed. However, basing the right to private ownership on labor is not a universalizable principle. The exclusive property of each has as its necessary corollary the privatization of others' property. Why, asks Proudhon, "is the benefit of this so-called law confined to a few and denied to the mass of labourers?" Accordingly, he challenges the owner who claims that the legitimacy of property derives from his labor: "You have laboured! Have you never made others labour? Why, then, have they lost in labouring for you what you have gained in not labouring for them?" A deadly question, to which Proudhon provides his famous response: "Property is theft! This is the warning bell of 93! The clamour of revolutions!"[44]

If the principles of liberty, equality, and security proclaimed by the revolutionary constitutions are absolute rights, then property is a right that, by contrast, stands outside and opposes society. If it is a natural right, then it is an "antisocial" one: "Property and society are completely irreconcilable with one another. It is as impossible to associate two proprietors as to join two magnets with their opposite poles. Either society must perish, or it must destroy property . . . In sum, property, after having robbed the labourer by usury, murders him slowly by starvation. Now, without robbery and murder, property cannot exist; with robbery and murder it soon dies for want of support. Therefore it is impossible."[45]

The critique of property is thus at the very birth and heart of all variants of socialism that arose in the nineteenth century in resistance to triumphant capitalism. It is not surprising then to find that Marx, led to take an interest in the topic for the first time by the Rhineland debates on the theft of wood, praises Proudhon's essay in *The Holy Family* as "a major scientific breakthrough," of comparable importance to him for modern politics as Siéyès's famous pamphlet on the third estate.

Possession and Property

The contradiction inherent in the idea of private appropriation effectively led Proudhon to establish a basic distinction between possession and property, and to challenge the historical transition from one to the other: "In order to change possession into property, something is needed besides labour, something without which a man would cease to be proprietor as soon as he ceased to be a labourer."[46] Implacable logic. The distinction between possession and property helps dispel the confusion attached to the double definition of property, as both "a domain and a possession." For jurists, possession is a fact; property is an institutionalized right. The argument that property rights are founded upon labor privatizes possession. By contrast, in primitive legislation, the metamorphosis of the possessor into proprietor was "legally impossible." The first farmers, who were the first lawyers, did not foresee "the consequences of the transformation of private possession into property." It was enough for them that their possession of the harvest was guaranteed. Everything would have started therefore with "continuous possession" and its perpetuation. For, "when the law declares that the lapse of time turns the possessor into a proprietor, it supposes that a right can be created without a cause that produces it." Law thus exceeds its powers: public order and the security of citizens requires only "a guarantee of possession."[47]

Moreover, even if recognized, the property of the producer over his product "does not mean property in the means of production; this seems to me to need no further demonstration. The soldier who possesses his arms, the mason who possesses the materials committed to his care, the fisherman who possesses the water, the hunter who possesses the fields and woods, and the cultivator who possesses the lands are all the same: all are, if you like, proprietors of their products, but none is proprietor of the means of production. The right to the produce is exclusively *jus in re*, the right to the means is common, *jus ad rem*."[48]

Marx often seems to take over the distinction between

possession and property. It was from this distinction that Paul Sereni, in a book of remarkable rigor, elucidates the mysteries of the distinction between private property and individual property contained in Book I of *Capital.* Sereni notes that, in the 1840s, "the dispute over property is really an extension and working out of the question of the predicate 'private' as an object of analysis." As early as *The German Ideology,* Marx and Engels point out that private property gradually became identified with property as such. It was thus transformed into an "abstract concept," permitting one to avoid having to say anything about "real private property." This ideological confusion hypostatizes the category of property and still serves today as the apologetic argument of the defenders of capital, making us believe that challenges to the private ownership of the means of production, exchange, and communication threaten individual possession. However, the private property that is subject to abolishment is only that "private and exclusive" form that Destutt de Tracy defines as that which "gives the power over work to others."[49]

Theft or Exploitation

In *The Holy Family,* Marx enthusiastically salutes Proudhon's essay. Their meeting in Paris nevertheless resulted in a rupture, consummated in 1847 by the sharp response of *The Poverty of Philosophy* to *The Philosophy of Poverty.* This was not the result of a change of mood between two men of incompatible temperaments but the result of Marx's theoretical maturation, which led to a much more elaborate critique of property, now enshrined in the communist perspective he gradually made his own.[50]

In *The Philosophy of Poverty,* Proudhon returns to the themes of *What Is Property?* He strives to incorporate a broader vision of political economy. It is, he writes, "the biggest problem that reason can pose," because property is "essentially contradictory." It combines the right of occupation and the right of exclusion, a price or reward for work and its negation for those one might call the nonpropertied *[les impropriétaires]*, a claim to justice and a legalization of theft. And with the development of credit, that prodigy of money that makes money, the speculator is enriched while he sleeps while the producer gets played. It combines the "fanaticism of competition" with the "fury of roulette." Certain passages from Proudhon have a strange contemporary resonance. Now, the producers "are known only as borrowers and money lenders, winners and losers": "Work has been blown away by the breath of credit, real value vanishes before fictive value, production falls before speculation . . . Credit releases capital in the end by releasing man from society and from nature. In this universal idealism, man no longer holds ground; he is suspended in the air by an invisible power."[51] Pushed to these ultimate conclusions, property reveals its "unsocial" character and discloses that, in its simplest expression, it is nothing more than the "right of force."

The theoretical dispute arises because, beginning with his Paris Manuscripts of 1844, Marx had undertaken to solve the mystery of surplus value and the accumulation of capital. His framework was turned upside down. The dispute focuses primarily on the illusion of equitable remuneration for work, based on its true value. For Marx, elementary individual work is at once social work, which presupposes a prior social accumulation of knowledge and expertise. While Proudhon opposed the virtues of original work to the misery of bonded labor—"real value" to "fictitious value," production to speculation—Marx discovered the contrary: the unity of concrete and abstract labor, of exchange- and use-value, the open secret of the commodity and the enchanted world of capital. While Proudhon contrasted the ideal of the small independent producer to "impersonal property" as "the worst form of property," Marx does not pine for these pastoral figures and considers as merely illusory the idea of reward at fair value, with good hours, for the work of each. Why? Because knowing whether "your hour of work is worth the same as mine is a question decided by competition!"

In other words, the price of the labor force cannot be determined a priori by the measure of its value, but only a posteriori by competition in the market: "What determines value is not the time in which a thing is actually produced, but the minimum time in which it is capable of being produced, and that is determined by competition."[52]

The alternative to the rule of capital imagined by Proudhon appears as a new chimera, parallel to the utopias he claims to fight. His "theory of mutuality," conceived as "a system of guarantees" that "turns competition into a benefit and monopoly into a guarantee of security for all," and his philanthropic call for a "sincere exchange" (today, one would say "fair") are at best nonsense and at worst an attempt to turn back the wheel of history. So it is not surprising if this theory of mutuality translates in practice into an apology for in-kind bartering and consumer lending, which is presented as a "synthesis of property and community."[53]

Marx's reply is scathing: "Troy has fallen. A fair proportion between supply and demand has long since ceased to exist." Previously, demand determined supply and preceded it: "production followed consumption step by step." Now "production precedes consumption, and supply drives demand." In the Proudhonian fantasy of equitable exchange, the costs of production would be expected to "determine the value of the product in all cases, and value would always be exchanged for equal worth." The labor of each individual would therefore be "the only measure of his profits and losses." An hour of Peter's work would simply be traded for an hour of Paul's: "this is the fundamental axiom of M. Bray." M. Proudhon's ranting replicates this pattern: "So if we suppose that all members of society were immediate producers, the exchange of equal amounts of hours is only possible if we all agree in advance the number of hours required in material production. But such an agreement denies individual exchange." Specifically, "social relations are not relations between one individual to another," but between worker and capitalist, farmer and landowner, and so on: "Wipe out these relations and you annihilate all society."[54]

In capitalist society, the question of property cannot be detached from the private appropriation of the surplus labor of others, that is, the issue of exploitation. Society is not reducible to an aggregation of individuals or "*immediate producers.*" It is a relation between antagonistic social classes. Even before the famous phrases of the *Communist Manifesto,* written at the end of the same year 1847, Marx summarizes in *The Poverty of Philosophy* the conflictual engine of historical change: "The very moment civilization begins, production begins to be founded on the antagonism of orders, estates, classes, and finally on that antagonism of accumulated labour and actual labour."[55] The practical conclusion he draws from this is the polar opposite of Proudhon. For Proudhon, "working coalitions" are as harmful as the corporations of the ancien régime and the fact that workers have "lost the habit" of them must be seen as progress.[56] For Marx, on the contrary, the mass of workers, "which is already a class against capital, but not yet for itself" gathers together in struggle and thereby "constitutes itself as a class for itself": "The interests it defends become class interests. But the struggle of class against class is a political struggle."[57]

In an article in 1865 on the occasion of Proudhon's death, Marx returns to his initial critique with greater clarity. Meanwhile, his framework has been considerably strengthened through the construction of *Capital.* He now considers the title of the 1840 essay on property as already indicative of its "inadequacy": "The question is so badly formulated it cannot be answered correctly . . . [H]istory itself had expressed its criticism upon past *property relations.* What Proudhon was actually dealing with was *modern bourgeois property* as it exists today. The question of what this is could have only been answered by a critical analysis of '*political economy*', embracing the totality of these *property relations,* considering not their *legal* aspect as *relations of violation* but their real form, that is, as *relations of production.*" As for *The Philosophy of Poverty,* Marx criticizes Proudhon for having shared in the "illusions of speculative philosophy": "Instead of regarding economic categories as the theoretical expression of historical relations of production, corresponding to a particular stage of development in material production, he garbles them into pre-existing eternal ideas, and how in this roundabout way he arrives once more at the standpoint of bourgeois economy."[58]

This radical critique leads to a rejection of the definition of property as theft, which remains a legal or moralistic conception: "In the best cases, bourgeois juridical notions of 'theft' are equally applicable to 'honest' profits. On the other hand, as theft, the violation of property *presupposes property*. Proudhon was embroiled in all sorts of confused ramblings about true bourgeois property." Instead of considering property an illegitimate legal category like most French socialists of the time, Marx's analysis, starting with *The German Ideology,* views it as a "necessary mode of relating to a stage in the development of productive forces." He thus came to relativize and secularize a notion of justice whose definition varies historically. There is therefore little sense in declaring exploitation unfair, or in denouncing property as theft, without greater precision. These are actually two conceptions of law that have come to clash, the rights of the property owners against the rights of the owned. Only force can decide between them.[59]

III.

THE CUSTOMARY RIGHT OF THE POOR TO THE COMMUNAL GOODS OF HUMANITY

In this period of market globalization and widespread privatization of the world, Marx's articles on the theft of wood are of troubling relevance. The purchase of the labor power of others establishes a relation of appropriation/expropriation, not only in the workforce but also in public services, public savings, consumption, bodies on display, and in space handed over to real estate and land speculation. Privatization affects not only public enterprises but also education, information, law (the generalization of private contract to the detriment of common law), money, knowledge, violence—in short, public space as a whole.

In his *Lectures on Industrial Society,* Raymond Aron liked to quote a passage from *Capital* where Marx says that "the dispersion of capital in large corporations already provides for the destruction of property," in order to conclude that "if dispersion equates to the elimination of private property, a large U.S. corporation is not private property." Despite the tales and legends of "popular capitalism" and beyond the apparent spread of property for the benefit of "employee ownership" and "small shareholders," concentration of ownership has reached unprecedented levels. In late 2003, global market capitalization reached thirty-one billion dollars, or nearly 90 percent of the world's gross domestic product. Shareholders now hold well over three-quarters of humanity's market wealth. If this wealth appears dispersed to the margins, it is in fact concentrated in a very small number of developed countries, so that 5 percent of the world's population (half of the United States) have almost all the world's stock holdings and seventy-seven thousand of the leading "ultrarich" alone hold approximately 15 percent of global wealth: "For many years, the population of the very rich grew much faster than that of the entire globe, and the expansion rate of their assets is higher than that of the global economy; in addition, the population growth of the ultra-rich is even faster: wealth inequality therefore tends to increase."[60]

To stifle the scandal of this monstrous private appropriation of natural and social wealth, the dominant discourse promises that everyone can become owners (of their own homes) or shareholders (of their businesses). It is not certain that the beneficiaries of "employee ownership" through shareholding truly feel as though they are the owners. It is likely, however, that their dual representation on boards of directors, as employees and as shareholders, will make them schizophrenic the day the dormant shareholder within will have to dismiss the employee within in order to ensure a return greater than 15 percent on investment. Other than imagining a financial version of the miracle of the loaves, the only way to achieve such a goal with a growth rate of under 3 percent is through the reduction of "labor costs." On this point at least, Proudhon was prescient, when he proclaimed the predictable cruelty of "impersonal property": "That which seems to soften and humanize property is precisely what reveals its hideousness: divided and impersonal property is its worst form."

The Privatization of Knowledge

Privatization aims at more than just natural resources or the products of work. It also desires knowledge and skills. This is what is at stake in the ongoing discussions and negotiations within the World Trade Organization on services, intellectual property, and patent law.[61] The traditional distinction between invention and discovery has been blurred, and the very limits of patentability have become problematic. Since the early 1980s, the need has emerged to legislate on scientific practices (such as the manipulation of life) in contrast to the definitions of property rights currently in force.

In the "new economy," a prototype created by research and development laboratories is often much more expensive in terms of fixed investment capital than the mass reproduction of the product. The acquisition of knowledge and the protection of the monopoly thus become the major issue in legislation on the new status of intellectual property. Yet *open science* is more favorable and "better adapted to the creation of new ideas than the market economy."[62] The privatization of research and its resulting knowledge, its sequestration away from competitors, the culture of secrecy and the pursuit of monopoly hinders the dissemination of socialized knowledge that could benefit the greatest number: "This contradiction reflects a twenty-first-century equivalent of what was in the last century a conflict between the public and private sector: the rivalry between 'free' and 'paying.' The temptation to download movies and songs, to circulate counterfeits, or manufacture generics is a permanent feature of the new economy, for the very reason that it costs little to duplicate the first unit of a product once it has been discovered."[63]

In 1992, the firm Agracetus obtained a patent not only on genetically modified cotton, but also on any change to the cotton gene in general, in other words, "on the very idea that one might modify the cotton gene." Through the course of the 1990s, we have seen the development of a logic of global enclosure. Such a development has major implications on research conditions.

The staggering proliferation of increasingly diverse patents that venture into the domain of research itself has turned the arena into a minefield of patents, left to patrol and limit not only the discoveries themselves but also areas of research and investigation likely to be made: "*Private Property! No entrance!*" Large firms have at their disposal a bank of litigious and argumentative troublemakers skilled at dissuading maverick researchers from risking venture into the thicket of costly litigation. "Changes have been so radical," says Dominique Pestre, "that there is now a movement underway toward the recollectivization of patents by large cartels who pool their patents to avoid having to constantly negotiate and slow down the innovation processes. Large companies allow each other to use the knowledge gained by each other. By contrast, for those not working within these cartel networks, it raises complex problems, in universities, for example." In fact, this recollectivization consists in a collective monopoly on the rents gained from brainpower, just like how energy cartels share oil revenue.[64]

Universities will be increasingly reduced, through private funding, to a subcontracting role in the service of these new knowledge cartels. There are already cases in Canada and the United States where the partnership agreement includes confidentiality clauses: the firm that subsidizes university research thus ensures exclusive control over the knowledge produced, to the detriment of its free circulation within the scientific community. These privacy clauses are not new. Previously, however, they were generally limited in time, pending filing and possible patenting, whereas they tend now to be permanent.[65] It is understandable that sincere or naive liberals end up being moved by it. All of this has nothing to do with "free and undistorted competition" anymore!

Reflecting on the ongoing debate in the United States on freedom, innovation, and the public domain, Grégoire Chamayou is justifiably surprised that critical resistance to intellectual property is no longer articulated in relation to that of traditional property. There is, of course, a certain specificity to the form of knowledge and the social production characteristic of intellectual property, but this is certainly not an "intellectual exception." France once boasted of having advanced "the cultural exception" in international trade negotiations, arguing that culture (cinema, literature, music . . .) is not a commodity like any another. Perhaps. But is health, education, or housing like other goods? In an age that wants to commodify everything, definitions and boundaries are uncertain. This is why battles around intellectual property can serve to reveal the contradictions inherent in the very idea of private property. As Grégoire Chamayou notes, "in a [liberal] conceptual context where property is linked to freedom, intellectual property is a paradoxical case where property comes to thwart freedom."[66] In property matters, is not this paradox the rule? At least that was what Proudhon was already trying to demonstrate.

Knowledge emerging from social practices was once confiscated and monopolized by the clergy or an upper caste. With industrial machinery, the appropriation of living work and its expertise acquired a new immediacy. With big industry, the whole range of sciences was, says Marx, "captured and put at the service of capital": "Historical development, political development, art, science, etc. . . . are located in the higher spheres above them. But it is only capital which has subjected historical progress to the service of wealth . . . At this point, invention becomes a business, and the application of science to immediate production itself becomes a factor determining and soliciting science." However, as big industry grows, "the creation of real wealth becomes less dependent upon labour time and the quantity of labour employed than upon the power of the agents set in motion during labour time. And their power—their POWERFUL EFFECTIVENESS—in turn bears no relation to the immediate labour time which their production costs, but depends, rather, upon the general level of development of science and the progress of technology, or on the application of science to production." Thus, "the *theft of alien labour time,* which is the basis of present wealth, appears to be a miserable foundation."[67] This miserable base is the reason for the disturbances of the world. The law of value can no longer measure the excesses of the world except at the price of ever-increasing global outbursts and violence.[68]

The Privatization of Life

In July 1998, the European Union authorized the grant of patents on "biological material": "An element isolated from the human body, or otherwise produced by a technical process, including the sequence or partial sequence of a gene, may constitute a patentable invention, even if the structure of that element is identical to that of a natural element."[69] Researchers do not "invent" a gene. Following the classic distinction, they are content to discover it. The boundary is becoming porous between the two notions, just as it is between the natural and the artificial. According to a director of industrial property at Aventis, invention would now consist in "assigning a technical function to the discovery sequence." Such broadening of the notion can lead very far. One can easily imagine how firms, pharmaceutical or other, could take advantage of this, and what interests are at stake in the patent battle.[70] We have a glimpse of this in the Myriad Genetics patent case on breast cancer screening tests. European institutions had developed cheaper and more reliable tests. Myriad objected to the marketing of these tests in the name of its property over "predisposition genes" and their uses. The European Patent Office, hit with numerous complaints, finally withdrew the firm's privileges.

A 1998 UN declaration equates the human genome with "the common heritage of humanity." In 2000, the G8 prohibited the patenting of gene sequences. The ongoing conflict between the logic of industrial (especially pharmaceutical) profitability and public health puts a redefinition of sharing between private and public on the agenda. Despite the agreement of specialists to patent the interpretation of the gene sequences, discomfort persists regarding the patenting of the sequences themselves. Accessible on the Internet, many biologists can now work on it. Patent law would pave the way for global judicial persecution of researchers who may, in good faith, violate patent-protected property rights. Here again, the contradiction between the private use of knowledge and its social character, connected at a cultural and technical level, is explosive.

The Common Good and the Freely Given

Controversies over multiple forms of patenting (including genome sequencing) thus revolve around a distinction between discovery and invention, and its legal interpretation. Can we privatize an idea, such as when software is basically only one element of applied logic, that is, a piece of "dead labor" that is built on accumulated intellectual work?[71] According to this logic of privative appropriation, could one go so far as to patent mathematical equations and subject them to property rights? The socialization of intellectual work begins with the practice of language, which is obviously a common social good of humanity that cannot be appropriated. Ongoing conflicts around intellectual property law tend to push hard against classic liberal notions of right and its legitimization of property through work.

These philosophico-legal puzzles are the result of contradictions between the growing socialization of intellectual labor and the private appropriation of ideas, on the one hand; between abstract labor, which underlies the market measure, and concrete work which is difficult to quantify, on the other. From these contradictions results a generalized disruption of the law of value as an increasingly *wretched* means by which to measure exchange and social wealth. Liberal economist Daniel Cohen recognizes that intellectual property "breaks with the pattern of property as a whole." A song or a chemical formula cannot be bought and consumed in the usual sense of the term. They survive the private use that is made of them. Buying a house or shoes amounts to claiming a legal monopoly over their use. Whereas property generally "makes possible the appropriation of an object," intellectual property "restricts it."[72]

"Free access to knowledge is a global public good."[73] Nevertheless, software patenting exploded in the 1990s in the United States, exceeding one hundred thousand. In this profusion, it becomes difficult, if not impossible, to publish software without being liable to counterfeiting. It is also becoming more and more difficult to distinguish the "software patent" from the "patent on intellectual method," to distinguish between technique and invention. Patenting thus reinforces industrial secrets and curbs innovation.[74] James Boyle draws an analogy between the "enclosures" at the time of primitive accumulation and these "new enclosures" of intellectual property.[75] Private land grabbing was defended at the time in the name of agrarian productivity, the increase of which was supposed to eradicate hunger and famine—even at the price of appalling urban misery. Today we are witnessing a "new wave of enclosures," justified in turn by the race for innovation or the exigencies of global food production. The differences between the two phenomena are not, however, insignificant. While the use of the land is mutually exclusive (what one appropriates, others cannot use), knowledge and expertise are "noncompetitive": the good does not go out of a gene sequence, software, or digital image when they are used. This is why, from the monastic scribe through to traditional printing, photocopying, and e-mail, the cost of reproduction has continued to decline. It is also why private appropriation is today justified by its role in the stimulation of research, rather than by the use of the product.

Is an algorithm an invention or a discovery? Alan Sokal recalls that most mathematicians consider any mathematical structure a discovery and not an invention, because the big book of nature is itself written in mathematical language. But even if an algorithm were considered an invention, its patenting would remain questionable: "Consider the inventor of an encryption algorithm used in all electronic transactions whenever anyone in the world uses his credit card. This is obviously a useful invention for which the inventor deserves to be paid, but does it deserve unlimited royalties? This problem already arose for traditional inventions, but it becomes more pressing for algorithms because they can be reproduced at almost zero cost." Initially, the principle behind the patent (and, in another form, that of the copyright) was to reward the inventor by granting him or her a limited-term monopoly, while promoting the circulation of knowledge now protected by the patent. However, the trend today is to accumulate preventive patents, extend their duration, and retain rather than circulate knowledge: firms can file patents on innovations that remained unused for the sole purpose of preventing them from being used by a competing firm.[76]

If computer science is a language, and if its innovations are patentable, can neologisms of everyday language become so? Concepts? Theories? To what unprecedented neuroses could this compulsion for intellectual property lead?! An outdated conception of appropriation is becoming more and more irrational and incompatible with the sharing of knowledge, to the point of becoming an obstacle to human development. Catherine Tasca, then French minister of culture and information, declared on July 10, 2000: "to avoid the risk of drying up creativity, we cannot carelessly render the work of the mind—an idea, a mathematical formula, software codes, a new formal expression—into the object of a patent." In that same year, marketing director at Microsoft France, Olivier Ezratty, declared himself in favor of a global harmonization of legislation: "Although we tend to place it under the model of research, characterized by a need to share knowledge, in fact, software creation is today an industrial process" that needs to be protected. He concluded: "We cannot encourage companies to create value if they cannot protect it."[77] The conflict of interest between social development and private interest couldn't be better described.

The principle behind free software records in its own way the highly cooperative character of intellectual labor, which is crystallized therein. The private monopoly of the owner is no longer contested, as in the case of liberals, in the name of the innovative virtue of competition, but rather as an obstacle to free cooperation. It is interesting to note the ambivalence of the English term "free" when applied to the software: liberty rhymes with availability.[78]

Inappropriable Goods

The extension of the commodification of the world to knowledge and life itself poses with new acuteness the question of the public good and the common good of humanity. The World Assembly of Legislators and Citizens for Water has set itself the goal of including access to water in the Universal Declaration of Human Rights.[79] As a "universal common good," water would then become "inappropriable." In 2006, the European Parliament unanimously adopted a resolution recognizing water as a human right. What works for water could do so for a number of other goods, be they natural or produced by the accumulated cooperative labor of many generations.

For Jean-Baptiste Say, arable land was "given free to man" and not created by him. Accordingly, it should be considered as part of the wealth of nature. However, the earth, being fixed, limited, and not "fugitive" like water, had become "a social resource whose use one had to pay for." Use? Of the products of the earth, or of the earth itself? Proudhon had already raised this thorny issue: "How can the goods of nature, the wealth created by Providence, become private property?" It is certainly easier to exercise an occupancy right over the land than the air, he replied, but "it is not a question of how easy something is." Say mistakes "opportunity for right." The question was not one of knowing why the land was more open to appropriation than the sea. Rather, "we only want to know by what right man has appropriated the wealth which he did not create and which was freely given to him by nature." Locke's argument, legitimizing property through labor, was turned against the proponents of the private appropriation of the common natural good: "But who made the land? God. Therefore, proprietor, retire."[80]

For Proudhon, "water, air and light are common things, not because they are inexhaustible, but because they are indispensable." Similarly, the earth, being indispensable to our conservation, is therefore inappropriable: "In two words, the equality of right is demonstrated by the equality of need." Therefore, like a "prophecy of equality" and a "republican oracle," "social sovereignty" conflicts with "individual property."

The ecological crisis is helping to put back on the agenda the idea of inappropriable common goods of humanity. Water is the best example, but the air has also become a disputed object with the establishment of a market on the right to pollute. And the land has never ceased to be so for agrarian movements fighting against land grabbing by large property owners. Land remains the focus of the struggles of the landless (in Brazil and elsewhere), but also of the new urban struggles: how will we face the urban crisis and the global explosion of slums, favelas, shantytowns, without "energetic incursions" into the sanctuary of private landed property and real estate?[81]

The "common good" no longer concerns only that which nature has supposedly "freely given" according to the classic argument of natural law. It is now equally relevant to human cooperative production. Proudhon already affirmed this: "Talent is a creation of society rather than a gift of nature; it is an accumulated capital of which the recipient is the guardian." For him, "just as the creation of every instrument of production is the result of collective force, so also the talent and knowledge of a man are the product of universal intelligence and general knowledge slowly accumulated by a number of masters and with the aid of many inferior industries." This is precisely the case with cognitive and cultural "capital": "as the traveller does not appropriate the highway which he travels, so the farmer does not appropriate the field which he cultivates . . . [A]ll capital, whether material or mental, is the result of collective labour and so is collective property . . . [A]nd since all capital is social property, no one has exclusive property of it."[82]

David Harvey defines capitalist globalization as a new phase of "accumulation by dispossession." He sees the continuation of the practices of "primitive" or "original" accumulation in force at the dawn of capitalism: "The reversion of common rights won through years of hard class struggle (the right to a state pension, to welfare, to national health care) into the private domain has been one of the most egregious of all policies of dispossession pursued in the name of neo-liberal orthodoxy."[83] This "accumulation by dispossession" is a condition of the survival of capitalism. Beyond the appropriation of raw materials, energy resources, cheap labor, it also includes the market appropriation of cultural history, notably through tourism, or even the pure and simple looting of cultural heritage. It uses various means, ranging from external coercion to the cannibalization by market logics of those forms of activity and production that still elude it (e.g., domestic work, human services, food production, etc.).

This offensive of neoliberal accumulation obviously involves the destruction of existing social rights and the criminalization of popular resistance (under the pretext of "antiterrorist" legislation). Thus we see a whole range of provisions that constitute a new kind of "poor law," aimed at strengthening social control and imposing a new discipline of flexible work through generalized precariousness.

In response, we are witnessing new forms of resistance of the dispossessed—those "*without*'"(without documents, homes, shelter, employment, or rights)—in the name of the defense of public services, in the name of the energy and food sovereignty of countries subject to imperialist looting, in the name of common goods (e.g., water, land, air, life) coveted by cannibalistic companies or pharmaceutical firms on the lookout for new patentable molecules. Or, simply, in the name of the right to have rights![84] Claims for the recognition of indigenous languages and cultures against standardizing globalization are part of this resistance to dispossession.[85] If these struggles are often initiated in the name of a defense of "habits and customs," or traditions, it is important to recall Marx's concern in his articles on the theft of wood. Behind the consensual appearance of custom resides the latent antagonism between the customary rights of the dominant and the dominated. This is perhaps what Walter Benjamin also understood when he juxtaposed the tradition of the oppressed to the conformity that always threatens it.[86]

Individual and Private Property

The 1842–43 articles on the theft of wood and on the situation of the Moselle vine growers were for Marx the starting point of a radical critique of private property in relation to the means of production and exchange. Five years later, in the *Communist Manifesto,* he made this question the touchstone of the nascent communist movement: "Communists can summarize their theory in this unique formula: the suppression of private property." This is why, in "all of their movements," they "put forward the question of property, to whatever degree of evolution it may have arrived, as the fundamental question of the movement." Accordingly, of the ten programmatic points that conclude the first chapter of the *Manifesto,* seven relate very directly to the forms of property.[87] They imply a primacy of "moral economics" over the competition of all against all, of solidarity over egoistic calculation, of the customary rights of the poor over the privilege of proprietors, of the public interest over private covetousness. It is not a question of abolishing all forms of property, just "the private property of today, bourgeois property," in other words "the mode of appropriation" that is based on the exploitation of the labor of others.

In *Capital,* Marx contrasts *individual* with *private* property: "The capitalist mode of appropriation, which springs from the capitalist mode of production, produces capitalist private property. This is the first negation of individual private property, as founded on the labor of its proprietor. But capitalist production begets, with the inexorability of a natural process, its own negation. This is the negation of the negation. It does not re-establish private property, but it does indeed establish individual property on the basis of the achievements of the capitalist era: namely co-operation and the possession in common of the land and the means of production produced by labour itself."[88]

Paul Sereni happily works to elucidate this enigmatic text. Marx recalls that among the Germanic tribes the *ager publicus*[89] is a mere complement to individual property. Each individual owner has then his share of the pasture, the hunting ground, or the common woods. The result is a historical distinction between individual and private property, and the identification of a type of property that does not tie the product to a single individual, cut off from the whole, the association, and the community. Sereni quotes the astonishing 1844 text in which Marx argues, "Let us suppose that we had carried out production as human beings . . . I would have the individual pleasure of knowing my personality to be *objective, visible to the senses,* and hence a power *beyond all doubt* . . . In your enjoyment or use of my product I would have the *direct* enjoyment both of being conscious of having satisfied a *human* need by my work, that is, of having objectified man's essential nature. In the individual expression of life I would have directly created your expression of your life, and therefore in my individual activity I would have directly *confirmed* and *realised* my true nature, my *human* nature, my *communal nature.* Our products would be so many mirrors in which we saw reflected our essential nature. This relationship would moreover be reciprocal; what occurs on my side has also to occur on yours."[90]

The contrast between individual and private property is repeated in *The Civil War in France.* There, Marx stresses that the Paris Commune "wants to make individual property a reality," and thus "restore" a form of appropriation that is genuine personal property. What does it mean, asks Sereni, to posit this restoration as the negation of the negation? He concludes that individualization in Marx is not the same as privatization. By reconciling the emancipation of each with that of all, the reestablishment of "individual property" becomes therefore compatible with social appropriation. But it is not, insists Marx, a simple return to an original community or some lost paradise. On the contrary, the "recovery" in question is based on the "acquisitions" or conquests of the capitalist era. What we are talking about is the emergence of a collectivity and a new individuality.

For Sereni, "the decisive point is the supposition that any form of self-realization can be called property." Marx would thus reconnect with another, original meaning of the notion of property, as used by Locke, for whom "every man is the owner of his own person," or by the Levellers who still saw in it the foundation of individual autonomy: "Marx appears to follow therefore the presupposition behind the idea of property in oneself."[91] This inalienable self-ownership would resist commodification in the labor force and would rebel and balk if required to offer itself on the labor market. As Marx writes in *Capital,* the "living personhood of a human being" will not resign itself to becoming a commodity like any other. This is why he evokes the perspective of a form of social appropriation that preserves "individual property" as self-realization. This implies more than a change in the legal status of property because, for him, social appropriation differs fundamentally from state ownership. From tirades against "vulgar communism" in the *Parisian Manuscripts of 1844* to the *Critique of the Gotha Program,* to his polemics with Lassalle, Marx never varied on this point. It is necessary to unpack all the consequences of the dispossession of the process and the product of work from the worker in terms of its effects on forced labor, commodity fetishism, and alienated work.[92] Owing to the "acquisitions" of capitalist development, the era of the private property of the individual worker is irredeemably lost, but an "individual form of possession in the broadest sense" remains the condition of the "free development of each": "Thus care of the self is central to communism and to its conception of individuality, so one must not ask whether there is a Marxist individualism, but rather in what sense it should be understood."[93]

The Age of Access?

Faced with widening inequalities and increasing exclusion, the new distribution of wealth becomes a social emergency. This is not simply about a more equitable distribution. The question is inextricably linked to that of property. Paradoxically, while privatization is in full swing and its concentration reaches an unparalleled level, there arises the strange idea that the issue of property is now part of the prehistory of the labor movement. Because licensing rights take precedence over the right of sale, providing license holders with a new form of rent, the question of property becomes soluble in shareholder salaries and the access economy.[94] Jeremy Rifkin, who had once imprudently ventured to prophesy "the end of labor," still argued in *The Age of Access* in 2000 that in the "new economy" property was doomed to give way to access, and the market would dissolve into the Internet. The market, however, is alive and well. To tame the Internet, the market simply needed to become networked. Hasn't it always been so? As for "access," it didn't replace property. Like all tolls, it is only a right of entry.[95]

In short, for Rifkin capital itself is being decapitalized. After "the end of labor," the end of capital? The two being closely intertwined, a common fate for them would have been logical. Their common survival is just as important. Nowadays we must work even harder, not to earn more, as Sarkozy's speeches would have us believe, but to pay more and live less. The more you work, the more capital prospers.

Jeremy Rifkin's ranting would be unimportant if it wasn't so revealing of the general trends in the early 2000s, in particular the new Blairist "Third Way" winds that were starting to blow over European social democracy. Prime Minister Lionel Jospin then glibly declared that "our industrial policy has gone beyond the question of the ownership of the means of production." He believed in it so much that he privatized on his own more than the right-wing governments (Balladur and Juppé) that had preceded him. As for Laurent Fabius, he crowed from the top of his roost in the National Assembly: "This problem [of the ownership of the means of production], despite its central role in the theory and practice of the Left in the twentieth century, is now behind us, even if, like starlight, we continue to discuss it long after the stars themselves have since disappeared."[96] Drawing out the conclusion to this audacious theoretical renovation, he announced with equal flourish that "all that is competitive is ultimately destined to be privatized." Judging by this energetic formula, the extension of privatization depends on what is deemed competitive; it is enough to decide that health or education should become competitive to infer that they should be privatized. Neither senile post-Stalinism, nor Mme Royal's social liberalism, nor Cohn-Bendit's eco-liberalism, nor Kouchner's humanitarian neocolonialism were especially moved by this hardy farewell to socialism.[97]

Contrary to leftists who have converted over to market euphoria, the economist Milton Friedman, the late leader of the ultraliberal school known as the Chicago boys (who have left more corpses in their wake than Al Capone and his henchmen), knew very well that property remains the heart of social war: "The crucial question is not whether the market will be played or not. All societies—communist, socialist, capitalist—use the market. The crucial question is that of private property."[98] Incidentally, Friedman thereby advised the fertile brains of Blair–Giddens's "Third Way" and Schröder–Hombart's "New Center" to "overcome the political obstacles to market expansion, to put an end to the 'tyranny of the status quo,' to 'discourage free-ridership and entitlement benefits.'"[99] There is no doubt that, from beyond the grave, this path inspired Sarkozy and his uninhibited right, just as it has the left-wing Italian coalition aligned behind Romano Prodi.

Enforcing Rights (against Existence)

The question of property and social appropriation permeates society. Under pressure from the Don Quixote Right to Housing public opinion campaign, in the fall of 2006 parliament passed a law establishing an "enforceable right" to housing.[100] Enforceable against whom or what? In theory, against public authorities, by providing legal recourse against public authorities if they are unable to provide housing to those who request it. However, this right to a roof over one's head conflicts with property rights—whether in the requisition of current residences, vacant housing, or sites for new building—such as when municipalities like Neuilly invoke their shortage to justify the absence of social housing on public land.

Among the ten objectives of Nicolas Hulot's Ecological Charter, signed by almost all the presidential candidates in a touching preelection consensus, was the goal of "containing suburban sprawl," "relocating human activities," and "establishing a true price on the services rendered by nature."[101] The desire for a harmonious balance between town and country is hardly new. It was already one of the ten priorities of the *Communist Manifesto* of 1848. It was also a major concern of Soviet village policy in the 1920s. It is true that the crisis of space is quite urgent today. The extension of transport increases pollution. Cities are being lost to shapeless, suburban wastelands. How can we imagine rebalancing this without affecting land ownership? Or without affecting real-estate speculation, which is driving the working underclass further and further out? More generally, how can we imagine a spatial revolution without social reappropriation?

Endeavoring to establish a "true price" for the services rendered by nature seems even more improbable. In order to establish their final price, the services in question must first be converted into a monetary value. This conversion presupposes an evaluation by the market, whose metabolism alone transforms qualitatively different goods and labor into abstract and commensurable values. But how can we evaluate in monetary terms the price that the planet pays for the burial of nuclear waste whose long-term effects are unpredictable? For deforestation? Ocean pollution? Melting glaciers? Climate change? Mercantile exchange and ecological development exist in different temporalities. The evaluation of the social cost of ecological disasters is not instantaneous, at the discretion of stock-market prices or the whims of the Dow Jones and CAC 40.[102]

Striving in seven hundred pages to quantify the costs of climate change, the Stern report on global warming has reached an approximate bill of 5,500 billion euros, including damage to urban infrastructure, health, and food production.[103] These forecasts can't pretend to incorporate the unforeseen long-term costs. The diagnosis is nevertheless categorical: climate change portends "unprecedented market failure"! Climatologists estimate the energy potential of solar radiation to be eight thousand times that of humanity's current needs and believe that currently available technology could already cover more than eight times these needs, provided there is a rapid transition to the new energy system. However, profits from oil, and the various interests tied to them, work in favor of vigorously maintaining the current "ecocidal" model. After the commodification of wood, coal, gas, and oil have all also become objects of exclusive appropriation. It would be difficult to make a diffuse and unlimited energy source such as solar power a similar source of profit.[104]

The Stern report compares the cost of inaction (waiting and leaving the market to it) with the cost of saving the climate, restricting itself as much as possible to the methods and criteria of market economics to do so. These accounting acrobatics convert things that are not commodities (e.g., human life, ecosystems) into that form, and then assign them a market price, which only illustrates the impossibility of solving the ecological challenge via the ruthless law of market value. With the support of scientific expertise and compassionate ethics, Nicholas Stern therefore recommends that governments drown social criticism of the ecological fracture in sermons on changing consumer behavior.

Social ecology has its own logic, which the madness of capitalism ignores. We cannot entrust the care of the planet to the shortsighted judgments of the stock exchange or the mechanisms of market regulation, even if it is a "green market," because we know very well that the competitive logic of capital stimulates the production of useless or harmful goods, demands expensive advertising campaigns, and generates overproduction and waste. The rather vague idea of "sustainable development" evokes a long and slow temporality, incompatible with hysteria in the race for capital gains or with the compulsive consumption incentivized by advertising. Between market logic, where abstract labor time is the standard for all things, and the reasoned relations of time and space characteristic of natural conditions for the reproduction of the human species, there is no common measure. The incommensurability between market values and ecological values marks one of the historical limits of the capitalist mode of production.

Faced with the cruelties of the market jungle, the Attac Manifesto outlines a series of measures meant to overthrow the pillars of neoliberalism.[105] But to attack these pillars is to call into question the sovereignty of property owners. Indeed, how can we plan for an ambitious, long-term program of energy conversion without challenging the power of the big oil companies or the nuclear industry, or without confronting the private lobbies of weapons manufacturers or the communications industry, which are more and more closely aligned? This is no longer about the comparative advantage of rational economic solutions. It is rather a test of political strength. Herein lies the distinction that makes all the difference. The resolution to defy the despotism of capital and markets is what separates a weak, minimal antiliberalism from one with real consequences. In other words, it defines an anticapitalist movement determined to change the world before it crushes us.

Who Will Win?

"Provided it is not taken in the narrow sense that it receives in the context of intellectual property law, nor reduced to a strictly formal conception of freedom of access, nor defended by 'differentialist' arguments, nor dissociated from the alternative forms of organizing production, the idea of the public domain can have an irreplaceable political significance," wrote Grégoire Chamayou.[106] These are many conditions, but they are those of an effective struggle against new forms of capitalist predation and accumulation. In the United States, some contest the fetishization of the term "public domain" on the grounds that its lexical unity covers very different situations. What is the relation between a copyright on a text and a patent on a molecule? To conflate these questions under the general heading of intellectual property, opposing it in an equally general manner to the idea of the public domain, may cause confusion: "It is true that the various issues gathered under these terms do not have the same degree of urgency nor the same actors. Still, I cannot rid myself of the idea that hackers who fight lockdowns on proprietary software, peasants who oppose technological control over seeds, internet users attached to the peer-to-peer model, scientists concerned with the ethics of sharing research results, librarians defending the principle of first sale against the taxation of reading, associations which oppose drug patents and the taxation of health, artists who think that all creation proceeds through sampling and collage of all sorts, autochthonous communities for whom the figure of the individual inventor has no meaning, and many others, are not unrelated. And perhaps the concept of 'public domain' could function to intensify these relations, which are as yet only attenuated."[107]

Through the debates on the theft of wood, Marx debarked in 1842 on the steep path toward the "critique of political economy," which led him to the heart of the mysteries and wonders of capital. From the customary right of the poor, passing through the principle of a "public domain" to the common heritage of humanity, the subject matter has changed but the question endures. Who will prevail: self-interested calculation or solidarity and common interest, property and an enforceable right to existence? Our lives are worth more than their profits: "Rise up, dispossessed of the world!"[108]

Proceedings of the Sixth Rhine Province Assembly, Third Article

Debates on the Law Concerning the Theft of Wood

KARL MARX

TRANSLATED BY ROBERT NICHOLS

Rheinische Zeitung, no. 298, October 25, 1842

We have so far described two of the most important state acts of the Provincial Assembly, namely, its confusion over freedom of the press and its bondage to that confusion.[1] We now come down to earth. Before we proceed to the really earthly question in all its life size, the question of the parceling out of landed property, we shall give our readers some genre images that in many ways reflect the spirit and, we might add, even the actual physical nature of the Assembly.[2]

It is true that the law on the theft of wood, like the law on offenses in regard to hunting, forests, and fields, deserves to be discussed not only in relation to the Assembly but also on its own terms. However, we do not have the draft of the law before us.[3] Our material is limited to some vaguely indicated additions made by the Assembly and its commission to laws that figure only as paragraph numbers. The Assembly proceedings themselves are so extremely sparsely, incoherently, and apocryphally[4] communicated that the report itself looks like an attempt at mystification. Judging by the truncated torso available to us, the Assembly wanted silence to pay an act of respect to our province.

One is immediately struck by one fact characteristic of these debates. The Assembly acts as a *supplementary legislator* alongside the state legislator. It will prove most interesting to examine the legislative qualities of the Assembly by way of an example. In view of this, the reader will forgive us for demanding from him patience and endurance, two virtues that have to be constantly exercised in analyzing our sterile subject matter. In our account of the Assembly debates on the law on theft we are directly describing the *Assembly's debates regarding its legislative function.*

At the very beginning of the debate, one of the urban deputies objected to the *title* of the law, which extends the category of *"theft"* to include simple offenses against forest regulations. A deputy of the knighthood replied: "It is precisely because the pilfering of wood is not regarded as theft that it occurs so often."[5] By analogy, the legislator would have to draw the following conclusion: It is because a slap is not regarded as murder that it has become so frequent. It should therefore be decreed that a slap is murder. Another deputy of the knighthood finds it "more dubious not to pronounce the word *theft* because people who become aware of this discussion could easily be led to believe that the Assembly does not regard the pilfering of wood as theft."

The Assembly has to decide whether it considers a violation of the woods [einen Holzfrevel] to be theft; but if the Assembly does not declare it to be so, people could believe that the Assembly really does not regard this violation to be theft. Hence it is best to leave this tricky, controversial question alone. It is a matter of euphemism and euphemisms should be avoided. The forest owner prevents the legislator from speaking, for walls have ears.

The same deputy goes even further. He regards this whole investigation into the term "theft" as "a questionable preoccupation with *editorial improvements* on the part of the plenary assembly." After these illuminating demonstrations, the Assembly voted to approve the title of the law.

From the point of view recommended above, which mistakes the conversion of a citizen into a thief for mere editorial negligence and rejects all opposition to it as grammatical purism, it is obvious that even the *pilfering of fallen wood* or the gathering of dry wood is included under the heading of theft and punished as severely as the stealing of live growing timber.

It is true that the above-mentioned urban deputy remarks: "Since punishment could lead to long-term imprisonment, such severity would lead otherwise honest people onto the path of crime. That would happen also because in prison they would be in the company of career criminals; he therefore considered that the gathering or pilfering of dry fallen wood should be punished by a simple police penalty." Another urban deputy, however, refuted him with the profound argument, "that in the forest areas of his region, at first only gashes were made in young trees, and later, when they were dead, they were treated as fallen wood."

It would be impossible to find a simpler or more elegant way to make the rights of human beings give way to those of young trees. On the one hand, after the adoption of the paragraph, it is inevitable that many people of a noncriminal disposition are cut off from the green tree of morality and, like fallen wood, are cast into the hell of crime, infamy, and misery. On the other hand, upon rejecting the paragraph, there is the possibility of the maltreatment of some young trees, and it needs hardly be said that human sacrifices will fall to victorious wooden idols!

The supreme penal code[6] subsumes under the category of theft only the pilfering of hewn wood and the cutting of wood for the purpose of stealing. And indeed, our Provincial Assembly will not believe it, stating: "If, however, in daytime someone takes fruit for eating and by its removal does no great damage, then, taking into account his personal position and the circumstances, he is to be punished by civil (therefore, not criminal!) 'proceedings.'"

The supreme penal code of the sixteenth century requests us to defend it against the charge of excessive humanity made by a Rhine Province Assembly of the nineteenth century, and we follow this request.

The gathering of fallen wood and the most composite wood theft! One provision is common to both. The appropriation of wood from someone else. Therefore, both are theft. This is summed up by the clear logic that has just passed laws. We must, therefore, first of all draw attention to the *difference* between them, and if one admits that the facts of the case are essentially different, it can hardly be maintained that they are the same in law.

In order to appropriate growing timber, it has to be forcibly separated from its organic connections. Because this is an open attack on the tree, it is therefore likewise an open attack on the owner of the tree. Further, if felled wood is stolen from a third party, the felled wood is a product of the owner. Felled wood is already formed wood. The natural connection with the property has been replaced by an artificial one. So, anyone who steals felled wood steals property. By contrast, when it comes to fallen wood, nothing has been separated from property. Only that which has already been separated from property is being removed. The wood thief issues a judgment against the property by his own authority. The gatherer of fallen wood only carries out a sentence already pronounced by the very nature of the property, for the owner possesses only the tree, but the tree no longer possesses the branches that have fallen from it. The gathering of fallen branches and the theft of wood are therefore essentially different things. The objects concerned are different, the actions in regard to them are no less different; hence the frame of mind must also be different, for what objective standard can be applied to the frame of mind other than the content and form of the action? But, in spite of this essential difference, you call both of them theft and punish both of them as such.[7] Indeed, you punish the gathering of fallen timber more severely than the actual theft of wood, for you punish the former already by declaring it to be theft, a punishment that you obviously do not pronounce on the latter. You should have called it murder of wood and punished it as murder. The law is not absolved from the general obligation to tell the truth. It is doubly obliged to do so, for it is the universal and authentic spokesman of the legal nature of things. The legal nature of things cannot therefore be regulated according to the law; on the contrary, the law must be regulated according to the legal nature of things. But if the law calls an act "theft" when it is scarcely even a violation of forest regulations, then the law *lies,* and the poor are sacrificed to a legal lie. As Montesquieu says, "There are two kinds of corruption: one, when the people do not observe the laws, the other, when they are corrupted by the laws; the latter is an incurable ill because it lies in the remedy itself."[8]

You will never succeed in making us believe that there is a crime where there is no crime, you will only succeed in converting crime itself into a legal act. You have blurred the boundaries between them, but you are wrong if you think they are blurred only to your advantage. People see the punishment, but they do not see the crime, and because they see punishment where there is no crime, they will see no crime where there is punishment. By applying the category of theft where it cannot be used, you have also glossed over where this category ought to be applied.

And does not this brutal view, which clings to a common definition for distinct kinds of action and disregards the differences between them, negate itself? If every infringement on property is termed theft, without distinction or a more exact definition, would not all private property be theft? Do I not exclude others from property through my private ownership? In doing so, do I not thereby infringe upon their ownership? If you deny the difference between essentially different kinds of the same crime, you deny that crime itself is *different from right,* so you abolish right itself, for every crime has an aspect in common with right. Hence it is a fact, attested equally by history and reason, that undifferentiated severity makes punishment wholly unsuccessful, for it has done away with punishment as a successful realization of right.

But what are we arguing about? The Assembly, it is true, rejects distinctions between the gathering of fallen wood, infringement of forest regulations, and theft of wood. It repudiates the difference between these actions, refusing to regard these distinctions as determinate of the character of the action, but only as this concerns the *interests of the infringers of forest regulations*; it recognizes this difference when it is a question of the *interests of the forest owners.*

Thus, the commission proposes the following *addition*: "to regard it as aggravating circumstances if growing timber is hewn or cut off with cutting tools and if a saw is used instead of an axe." The Assembly approves this distinction. The same ingenuity, which so scrupulously distinguishes between an axe and a saw when it is a matter of its own interests, is so lacking in conscience as to refuse to distinguish between fallen wood and growing timber when it is a question of other people's interests. The difference was found to be significant as an aggravating circumstance but of no importance as a mitigating circumstance, although the former cannot exist if the latter is impossible.

The same logic occurred repeatedly during the debate. In regard to §65, an urban deputy desired "that the *value* of the stolen wood should also be used as a measure for determining the punishment," "which was opposed by the commission's spokesman as *unpractical*." The same urban deputy remarked in connection with §66: "in general there is missing from the whole law any indication of value, in accordance with which the punishment would be increased or decreased." The importance of value in determining punishment for violations of property is self-evident.

If the concept of crime involves that of punishment, the reality of crime calls for a measure of punishment. Real crime is limited. Punishment will therefore have to be limited in order to be actual; it must be limited in accordance with a principle of law in order to be just. The task is to make the punishment be the real consequence of the crime. It must be seen by the criminal as the necessary effect of his act, and therefore as his own act. Hence the limit of his punishment must be the limit of his act. The definite *content* of a violation of the law is the limit of a definite crime. The *measure* of this content is therefore the measure of the crime. In the case of property this measure is its *value*. Whereas personality, whatever its limits, is always a whole, property always exists only within a definite limit that is not only determinable but determined, not only measurable but measured. Value is the civil mode of existence of property, the logical expression through which it first becomes socially intelligible and communicable.[9] It is clear that this objective determination, given by the nature of the object itself, must likewise be the objective and essential defining element of the punishment. Where it is a matter of figures, the legislation can here only proceed by external features in order not to become lost in the endlessness of determination, because it must at least regulate things. It is not a question of an exhaustive definition of differences, but of establishing differences. It does not matter that the differences be exhausted; what matters is that they are made. But the Assembly did not even care enough to pay attention to such trivial matters.

Do you now believe that it is possible to conclude that the Assembly completely excluded value in determining punishment? That would be a careless, impractical conclusion! The forest owner—we shall deal with this later in more detail—does not merely demand to be compensated by the thief for the simple general value. He even gives this value an individual character and bases his claim for special compensation on this poetic individuality. We can now understand what the commission's spokesman understands by *practical.* The practical forest owner argues as follows: This legal definition is good insofar as it is useful to me, for what is useful to me is good. But this legal definition is superfluous, it is harmful, it is unpractical, insofar as it is intended to be applied to the accused on the basis of a purely theoretical legal whim. Because the defendant is harmful to me, it stands to reason that everything is harmful to me that diminishes the harm coming to him. That is practical wisdom.

We unpractical people, however, demand for the poor, politically and socially propertyless multitude what the learned and teachable servility of the so-called historians has discovered to be the true philosopher's stone for turning every unfair presumption into the pure gold of right. We demand for the poor a *customary right,* and indeed not one that is only of a local character, but is a customary right of the poor in all countries. We go still further and maintain that a customary right by its very nature can only be a right of this lowest, propertyless, and elemental mass.

The so-called customs of the privileged classes are understood to mean *customs contrary to the law.* Their origin dates to the period in which human history was part of *natural history,* and in which, according to Egyptian myth, all the gods hid themselves in animal form. Humanity appeared to fall into definite species of animals that were connected not by equality, but by inequality, an inequality fixed by laws. The world condition of unfreedom required laws expressing this unfreedom, for whereas human law is the mode of existence of freedom, this animal law is the mode of existence of unfreedom. *Feudalism* in the broadest sense is the *spiritual animal kingdom,* the world of divided mankind, in contrast to the human world that creates its own distinctions and whose inequality is nothing but a refracted form of equality. In the countries of naive feudalism, in the countries of the caste system, where in the literal sense of the word people are put in separate boxes[10] and the noble, freely interchanging members of the great sacred body, the holy Humanus, are sawn, wedged, torn apart by force, we find therefore also the *worship of animals,* animal religion in its primitive form, for man always regards as his highest being that which is his true being. The sole equality to be found in the real life of animals is the equality between an animal and others of the same species; it is the equality of the given species with itself, but not the equality of the genus. The animal genus itself is seen only in the hostile behavior of the different animal species, which assert their particular *distinctive* characteristics one against another. In the *stomach of the predator,* nature has provided its chosen site for union, the crucible of intimate fusion, the organ connecting the various animal species. Likewise, in feudalism one species feeds at the expense of another, right down to the species that, like the polyp, grows on the ground and has only numerous arms with which to pluck the fruits of the earth for higher races while it itself eats dust; for whereas in the natural animal kingdom the worker bees kill the drones, in the spiritual animal kingdom the drones kill the worker bees, and precisely by labor. When the privileged classes appeal from *legal right* to their *customary rights,* they are demanding, instead of the human content of right, its animal form. Right has now become a mere animal mask.

Rheinische Zeitung, no. 300, October 27, 1842

The customary rights of the aristocracy conflict by their *content* with the form of universal law. They cannot be given the form of law because they are formations of lawlessness. The fact that their content is contrary to the form of law—universality and necessity—proves that they are *customary wrongs* and cannot be asserted in opposition to the law. Rather, whenever such opposition arises, they must be abolished and even punished if the occasion arises, for no one's action ceases to be wrongful because it is his custom, just as the marauding son of a robber is not exonerated because banditry is a family idiosyncrasy. If someone intentionally acts contrary to law, he is punished for his intention; if he acts by custom, this custom of his is punished as a bad custom. At a time when universal laws prevail, rational customary right is nothing but the *custom of legal right,* for right has not ceased to be custom because it has been embodied in law, although it has ceased to be *merely* custom. For one who acts in accordance with right, right becomes his own custom, but it is enforced against one who violates it, although it is not his custom. Right no longer depends on chance, on whether custom is rational or not, but custom becomes rational because right is legal, because custom has become the custom of the state.

Customary right as a *separate domain* alongside legal right is therefore rational only where it exists *alongside* and *in addition to law,* where custom is the *anticipation* of a legal right. Hence one cannot speak of the customary rights of the privileged estates. They have found in the law not only a recognition of their rational right, but often even of their irrational pretensions. They have no right to anticipate contrary to the law, for the law has anticipated all the possible consequences of their right. Their customary rights are therefore only required in the domain of *menus plaisirs*, so that the same content which is treated in the law according to its rational limits should find leeway in custom for the whims and pretensions beyond these rational limits.[11]

But whereas these customary rights of the aristocracy are

contrary to the conception of rational right, the customary rights of the poor are rights contrary to the customs of positive law. Their content does not conflict with legal form, but rather with its own formlessness. The form of law is not in contradiction to this content; on the contrary, the latter has not yet reached this form. It requires little reflection to perceive how *one-sidedly* enlightened legislation has treated and been compelled to treat the *customary rights of the poor,* of which the various *Germanic* rights can be considered the most prolific source.[12]

The most liberal legislations have been confined in *civil law* to formulating and raising to a universal level those rights already found to exist. Where they did not find any such rights, neither did they create any. They abolished particular customs, but in so doing forgot that whereas the wrong of the estates took the form of arbitrary pretensions, the right of those without social estate appeared in the form of accidental concessions. This course of action was correct in regard to those who, besides right, enjoyed custom, but it was incorrect in regard to those who had only customs without rights. Just as these legislations converted arbitrary pretensions into legal claims, insofar as some rational content of right was to be found in those pretensions, they ought also to have converted accidental concessions into necessary ones. We can make this clear by taking the monasteries as an example. The monasteries were abolished, their property was secularized, and it was right to do so. But the fortuitous support the poor found in the monasteries was by no means replaced by any other positive source of income. When the property of the monasteries was converted into private property, the monasteries themselves received some compensation but the poor who lived by them did not. On the contrary, at the same time as they were deprived of an ancient right, a new restriction was imposed on them. This occurred in all transformations of privileges into rights. A positive aspect of these abuses—which was also an abuse because it turned a right of one side into something accidental—was abolished not by the accidental being converted into a necessity, but by its being left out of consideration.

These legislations were necessarily one-sided, for all customary rights of the poor were based on the fact that certain forms of property were indeterminate in character, neither definitely private property nor definitely common property, but a mixture of private and public right, such as we find in all the institutions of the Middle Ages. For the purpose of legislation, such ambiguous forms could be grasped only by understanding, and understanding is not only one-sided, but has the essential function of making the world one-sided, a great and remarkable work, for only one-sidedness can extract the particular from the unorganized mass of the whole and give it shape. The character of a thing is a product of understanding. Each thing must isolate itself and become isolated in order to be something. By confining each of the contents of the world in a stable definiteness and as it were solidifying the fluid essence of this content, understanding brings out the manifold diversity of the world, for the world would not be many-sided without the many one-sidednesses.

Understanding therefore abolished the hybrid, indeterminate forms of property by applying to them the existing categories of abstract civil law, the model for which was found in Roman law. The legislative mind considered it was more justified in abolishing the obligations of this indeterminate property toward the poorer class because it also abolished state privileges of property. It forgot, however, that even within civil law there exists a twofold private right: a private right of the owner and a private right of the nonowner. Moreover, no legislation abolishes the privileges of property under constitutional law, but merely divests them of their more venturesome character and gives them instead a civil character. If, however, every medieval form of right, and therefore of property also, was in every respect hybrid, dualistic, split into two, and understanding rightly asserted its principle of unity in respect of this contradictory determination, it nevertheless overlooked the fact that there exist objects of property that, by their very nature, can never acquire the character of predetermined private property, objects that, by their elemental nature and their accidental mode of existence, belong to the sphere of occupation rights, and therefore of the occupation right of that class which, precisely because of these occupation rights, is excluded from all other property and which has the same position in civil society as these objects have in nature.

It will be found that the customs that are customs of the entire poor class are based on their instinctive grasp of the *indeterminate* aspect of property; it will be found not only that this class feels an urge to satisfy a natural need, but equally that it feels the need to satisfy a rightful urge. Fallen wood serves as an example. Such wood has as little organic connection with the growing tree as shed skin has with the snake. Nature itself presents as it were a model of the antithesis between poverty and wealth in the shape of the dry, snapped twigs and branches separated from organic life in contrast to the trees and stems that are firmly rooted and full of sap, organically assimilating air, light, water, and soil to develop their own proper form and individual life. It is a physical representation of poverty and wealth. Human poverty feels this kinship and derives its right to property from it. If, therefore, it claims physical organic wealth for the predetermined property owners, it claims physical poverty for need and chance. In this play of elemental forces, poverty senses a friendly power more humane than human power. The fortuitous arbitrary chance of privileged individuals is replaced by the fortuitous operation of elemental forces, which take away from private property what the latter no longer voluntarily releases. Just as it is not fitting for the rich to lay claim to alms distributed in the street, so too with regard to these *alms of nature*. But it is by its *activity,* too, that poverty acquires its right. By its act of *gathering,* the elemental class of human society appoints itself to introduce order among the products of the elemental power of nature. The position is similar in regard to those products that, because of their wild growth, are a wholly accidental appendage of property and, if only because of their insignificance, are not objects for the activity of the actual owner. The same holds true in regard to postharvest gleaning and other similar customary rights. Thus, an instinctive sense of justice lives in these customs of the poor. Its root is positive and legitimate, and the form of *customary right* here conforms all the more to nature because up to now the *existence of the poor class itself* has been a *mere custom* of civil society, a custom that has not found an appropriate place in the conscious organization of the state.

The present debate immediately presents an example of how to treat these customary rights, an example that exhaustively illustrates the method and spirit of the whole procedure.

An urban deputy opposed the provision by which the gathering of wild berries and cranberries is treated as theft. He spoke primarily on behalf of the children of the poor, who pick these fruits to earn a little something for their parents—an activity that has been permitted by the owners *since time immemorial* and has given rise to a *customary right* of the children. This fact was countered by another deputy, who remarked that "in his area these berries are already commodities and would be sent to Holland by the barrel."

In *one locality,* therefore, things have been brought to a turning point such that the customary right of the poor has been converted into a *monopoly* of the rich. That is exhaustive proof that common property can be monopolized, from which it naturally follows that it must be monopolized. The nature of the object calls for monopoly because private-property interests here have invented this monopoly. The modern idea conceived by some money-grabbing petty traders becomes irrefutable when it provides profit for the age-old Teutonic landed interest.

The wise legislator will prevent crime in order not to have to punish it, but he will do so not by obstructing the sphere of right, but by doing away with the negative aspect of every instinct of right, giving the latter a positive sphere of action. He will not confine himself to removing the *impossibility* for members of one class to belong to a higher sphere of right, but will raise their class itself to the *real possibility* of enjoying its rights. But if the state is not humane, rich, and high-minded enough for this, it is at least the legislator's absolute duty not to convert into a crime what circumstances alone have caused to be an *offense.*[13]

He must exercise utmost leniency in correcting as a social *irregularity* what would be the height of injustice for him to punish as an antisocial crime. Otherwise he will be combating social instinct while supposing that he is combating its antisocial form. In short, if popular customary rights are suppressed, the attempt to exercise them can only be treated as the simple *contravention of a police regulation,* but never punished as a crime. Police punishment is a solution to an act that has been stamped superficially by circumstances as disorderly, but which does not constitute a violation of the eternal rule of law. The punishment must not inspire more repugnance than the offense, the ignominy of crime must not be turned into the ignominy of law; the basis of the state is undermined if misfortune becomes a crime or crime becomes a misfortune. Far from upholding this point of view, the Provincial Assembly does not observe even the elementary rules of legislation.

The petty, wooden, mindless, and selfish soul of interest sees only one point, the point where it is injured, like a coarse person who regards a passerby as the most infamous, vilest creature under the sun because this unfortunate creature has trodden on his corns. He makes his calluses the basis for his views and judgment; he makes the one point where the passerby comes into contact with him into the only point where the very essence of this man comes into contact with the world. But a man may very well happen to tread on my corns without ceasing to be an honest, even excellent, man. Just as you must not judge people by your corns, you must not see them through the eyes of your private interest.[14] Private interest makes the one sphere in which a person comes into conflict with this interest into this person's whole sphere of life. It makes the law a *rat catcher,* who wants only to destroy vermin, for he is not a naturalist and therefore regards rats only as vermin. But the state must regard the infringer of forest regulations as something more than a wood-pilferer, more than an *enemy to wood.* Is not the state linked with each of its citizens by a thousand vital nerves, and has it the right to sever all these nerves because this citizen has himself arbitrarily severed *one* of them? Therefore the state will regard even an infringer of forest regulations as a human being, a living member of the state, one in whom its heart's blood flows, a soldier who has to defend his homeland, a witness whose voice must be heard by the court, a community member with public duties to perform, the father of a family, whose existence is sacred, and, above all, a citizen of the state. The state will not recklessly exclude one of its members from all these functions, for the state amputates itself whenever it turns a citizen into a criminal. Above all, however, the *moral* legislator will consider it a most serious, painful, and dangerous matter to subsume under the sphere of crime that which was previously regarded as innocent.

Interest, however, is practical, and nothing in the world is more practical than to strike down one's enemy. "Hates any man the thing he would not kill?" we are already told by Shylock.[15] The true legislator should fear nothing but injustice, but the legislative interest knows only fear of the consequences of rights, fear of the evildoers against whom the laws are made. Cruelty is a characteristic feature of laws dictated by cowardice, for cowardice can be energetic only by being cruel. Private interest, however, is always cowardly, for its heart, its soul, is an external object that can always be wrenched away and injured, and who has not trembled at the danger of losing heart and soul? How could the selfish legislator be human when something inhuman, an alien material essence, is his highest essence? *"Quand il a peur, il est terrible,"*[16] says the *National* about Guizot. These words could be inscribed as a motto over all *legislation inspired by self-interest,* and therefore by *cowardice.*[17]

When the Samoyeds kill an animal, before skinning it they assure it in the most serious tones that only Russians have done it this injury, that it is being dismembered with a Russian knife, and therefore it should avenge itself only on Russians. Even without any claim to be a Samoyed, it is possible to turn the law into a *Russian knife.* Let us see how this is done.

In §4, the commission proposed: "At distances greater than two miles, the *warden who makes the charge* determines the *value* according to the existing local price." An urban deputy protested against this as follows:

> The proposal to allow the valuation of the stolen wood to be made by the forester who brings the complaint would be very questionable. Of course, this official has our full confidence, but only as regards the fact, not the value. The latter should be determined according to a valuation made by the local authorities and confirmed by the district administrator. It is proposed, however, that §14, according to which the penalty imposed should accrue to the forest owner, should not be adopted," etc. "If one were to maintain §14, the present provision would be doubly dangerous. For the forester, who is in the service of the forest owner and paid by him, must, by the nature of the circumstances he is in, set the value of the stolen wood as high as possible.

The Provincial Assembly approved the proposal of the commission.

We see here the enactment of patrimonial jurisdiction. The patrimonial warden is at the same time in part a judge. The valuation forms part of the sentence. Hence the sentence is already partly anticipated in the record of the charge. The warden who made the charge sits on the court; he is the expert whose decision is binding for the court, someone who performs a function that excludes other judges. It is foolish to oppose the inquisitorial process when the patrimonial gendarmes and denouncers are also the judges.

Apart from this fundamental violation of our institutions, it is obvious from an examination of the qualifications of the warden who makes the charge how little he is objectively able to be at the same time the one who places a value on the stolen wood.

As warden, he is the personified guardian of the woods. Protection, especially personal, physical protection, calls for an effective, energetic, and loving attitude to the object of his care, an attitude whereby his growth and that of the forest converge. The forest must be everything to him, it must be of absolute value to him. The appraiser of the stolen wood, on the other hand, behaves with skeptical mistrust. He measures it with a sharp prosaic eye according to an ordinary standard and determines how much it is worth down to the last penny. A warden and an appraiser are as different as a mineralogist and a trader in minerals. The forest warden cannot estimate the value of the stolen wood, for in any record for the court giving his estimate of the value of the stolen material he is estimating *his own value,* because it is the value of his own activity, and do you believe that he would not protect the *value* of the object under his care as much as the *substance* of it?

The functions entrusted to one man, for whom severity is an official duty, are contradictory not only in relation to the object under protection, but also in relation to the *persons* concerned.

As guardian of the wood, the warden should protect the interests of the private owner. As appraiser, however, he should also protect the interests of those who would infringe upon forest regulations against the extravagant demands of the private owner. While he has, perhaps, to use his fists on behalf of the forest, he has just as quickly to use his brains on behalf of the forest's enemy. While acting as the embodied interest of the forest owner, he has at the same time to be a guarantee against these same interests.

The warden, furthermore, is the informant. The protocol is a denunciation. The value of the object, therefore, becomes the subject matter of the denunciation. The warden loses his dignity as a judge, and the function of judge is most profoundly debased, because at that moment it is indistinguishable from the function of informant.

Finally, this denouncing warden, who is not suitably positioned to serve as either an expert informant or a guard, is in the pay and service of the forest owner. One might just as well leave the appraising, under oath, to the forest owner himself, because in the person of his warden he has actually only assumed the shape of a third person.

Instead, however, of questioning this position of the denouncing warden as problematic, on the contrary, the Provincial Assembly questioned the only provision that constituted the last semblance of the state's power in the realm of forest glory, namely, the *lifetime appointment* of the denouncing wardens. This proposal evoked the most vehement protest, and the storm seems hardly to have been abated by the explanation of the proponents "that previous Provincial Assemblies had already called for the repeal of lifetime appointment for wardens, but that the government had not agreed to this and regarded life appointment as a protection for the state's subjects."

The Provincial Assembly had therefore already tried to bargain with the government so as to make it abandon protection for its subjects, a negotiation it never gave up on. Let us examine the arguments, as generous as they are irrefutable, advanced *against* life appointment.

A deputy from the rural communities "finds that establishing life appointments for wardens as a condition for confidence in them undermines the position of small forest owners; and another deputy insists that protection must be equally effective for small and big forest owners."

A member of the princely estate remarked that "life appointments for private persons is very unreasonable, and in France it has not been found at all necessary for ensuring confidence in the records drawn up by the wardens, but that something must of necessity be done to prevent infringements from increasing."

An *urban deputy* said:

> All reports from properly appointed and sworn forest officials must be given credence. Lifetime appointment is virtually impossible for many communities, especially for owners of small estates. Deciding that only forest officials who have been appointed for life should be trusted would deprive these owners of all forest protection. In a large part of the province, communities and private owners would necessarily have to entrust the protection of their wooded

areas to field wardens, because their forest area is not large enough to enable them to appoint special foresters for it. It would indeed be strange if these field wardens, who have also taken an oath to protect the forests, were not to enjoy complete confidence when they reported a theft of wood, but were trusted when they testified to the infringement of forest regulations.

Rheinische Zeitung, no. 303, October 30, 1842

Thus *town* and *countryside* and the *princely estate* have had their say. Instead of smoothing out the difference between the rights of the infringer of forest regulations and the claims of the forest owner, they found that this difference was not great enough. There was no attempt to afford equal protection to the forest owner and the infringer of forest regulations, only equal protection for small and large forest owners. In the latter, legal equality is measured down to the minutest detail, while in the former inequality is an axiom. Why does the small forest owner demand the same protection as the big forest owner? Because both are forest owners. But are not both the forest owners and the infringers of forest regulations citizens of the state? If small and big forest owners have the same right to protection by the state, does this not apply even more so to small and big citizens of the state?

When the member of the princely estate refers to France—for interest knows no political antipathies—he only forgets to add that in France the warden's charge concerns only the facts of the case, not the value. Similarly, the honorable urban spokesman forgets that it is inadmissible to rely on a field warden here because it is a matter not only of registering a theft of wood but also of establishing the value of the wood.

What is the core of the entire reasoning we have just heard? It is that the small forest owner does not have the *means* for appointing a warden for life. What follows from this? It follows that the small forest owner is not entitled to undertake this task.

What does the small forest owner conclude from this? That he is entitled to appoint as an appraiser a warden who can be dismissed. His lack of means entitles him to a privilege.

Nor does the small forest owner have the means to support an independent *judicial college*. Therefore, let the state and the accused manage without an independent one; let a manservant of the small forest owner have a seat on the bench, or if he has no manservant, let it be his maid; and if he has no maid, let him sit there himself. Does the accused not have the same right to the executive power, which is an organ of the state, as he has in regard to the judicial power? So why not set up the court according to the means of the small forest owner?

Can the relation between the state and the defendant be altered because of the scarce resources of a private person, the forest owner? The state has a right in relation to the accused because it confronts him as the state. An immediate consequence of this is its duty to act toward the lawbreaker as a state and in the manner of a state. The state not only has the means to act in a way that is as appropriate to its reason, its universality, and its dignity as it is to the right, the life, and the property of the incriminated citizen; it is its absolute duty to have and make use of these means. No one will make this demand of the forest owner, whose forest is not the state and whose soul is not the soul of the state. But what conclusion was drawn from that? That, because private property does not have the means to raise itself to the standpoint of the state, the state is obliged to lower itself to the irrational and illegal means of private property.

This claim on the part of private interest, whose meager soul was never enlightened and sparked by thought of the state, is a serious and thorough lesson for the state. If the state stoops so low, even at one point as to act in the manner of private property instead of in its own way, it follows immediately from this that it has to adapt itself in the form of its means to the narrow limits of private property. Private interest is clever enough to magnify this consequence to the point where private interest, in its most restricted and paltry form, makes itself the limit and rule for state action. As a result of this, apart from the complete degradation of the state, we have the reverse effect that the most irrational and illegal means are put into operation against the accused; supreme concern for the interests of limited private property necessarily turns into total disregard for the interests of the accused. If, however, it becomes clearly evident here that private interest seeks to degrade, and is bound to degrade, the state into a means operating to its own benefit, how can it fail to follow that a *body representing private interests,* the estates, will seek to degrade, and is bound to degrade, the state to the idea of private interest? Every modern state, however little it corresponds to its concept, will be forced at the first practical attempt at such legislative power to exclaim: Your ways are not my ways, your thoughts are not my thoughts![18]

How completely untenable then is the temporary hiring of a denouncing warden, which couldn't be made more obvious than by an argument advanced *against* lifetime appointments, and which cannot be attributed to a slip of the tongue, for it was read out. Namely, the following remark was read out by an urban deputy:

> Community forest wardens appointed for life are not, and cannot be, under such strict control as royal officials. Every *spur* to loyal fulfillment of duty is *paralyzed* by lifetime appointment. If the forest warden only half performs his duty and takes care that he cannot be charged with any real offense, he will always find sufficient advocacy in his favor to make a proposal for his dismissal under §56 useless. In such circumstances the interested parties will not even dare to put forward such a proposal.

We recall how the warden making the charge was given full confidence when it came to the task of appraisal. We recall that §4 was a *vote of confidence* in the warden. We now learn for the first time that the denouncing warden needs to be controlled, and strictly so. For the first time he appears not merely as a man, but as a horse, because the carrot and the stick are the only stimuli of his conscience, and the muscles for performing his duty are not merely slackened but completely paralyzed by life appointment. We see that selfishness has a double set of weights and measures for weighing and measuring people, and two worldviews, two pairs of spectacles, one showing everything black and the other rose-colored. When it is a matter of making other people the victim of its tools and whitewashing dubious means, selfishness puts on its rose-colored spectacles, which give an imaginary glory to these tools and means, and deludes itself and others with the unpractical, delightful dreaming of a tender and trusting soul. Every wrinkle of its face is smiling bonhomie. It presses its opponent's hand until it hurts, but it does so as a sign of its trust in him. But all of a sudden it takes personal advantage, it is behind the scenes, where the illusions of the stage disappear, where it can carefully examine the usefulness of its tools and means. Being a strict judge of people, it cautiously and suspiciously puts on its worldly-wise black glasses of practice. Like an experienced horse dealer, it subjects people to a lengthy ocular inspection, overlooking no detail, and they seem to it to be as petty, as pitiful, and as dirty as selfishness itself.

We do not want to argue with the selfish worldview, but we want to force it to be consistent. We do not want it to reserve all worldly wisdom for itself and leave only fantasies for others. We want to make the sophistic spirit of private interest abide for a moment by its own conclusions.

If the warden making the charge is a man such as you describe, a man whom lifetime appointment, far from giving him a feeling of independence, security, and dignity in the performance of his duty, has, on the contrary, deprived him of any incentive to do his duty, how can we expect this man to behave impartially toward the accused when he is the unconditional slave of your arbitrary power? If only spurs can compel this man to his duty, and if you are the wearer of the spurs, what fate must we prophesy for the accused, who wears no spurs? If even you yourself cannot exercise sufficiently strict control over this warden, how can the state or the accused control him? Does not what you say of lifetime appointment apply instead to an appointment that can be terminated: "if the forest warden only half performs his duty . . . , he will always find sufficient advocacy in his favor to make a proposal for his dismissal under §56 useless"? Would not all of you be advocates for him as long as he performed half his duty, namely, the protection of your interests?

The transformation of the naive, overflowing confidence in the forest warden into abusive, censorious distrust reveals the heart of the matter. It is not in the forest warden but in yourselves that you place this tremendous confidence, which you want the state and the infringer of forest regulations alike to accept as dogma.

It is not the warden's official position, nor his oath, nor his conscience that should be the guarantee of the accused against you; on the contrary, your sense of justice, your humanity, your disinterestedness, your moderation should be the guarantee of the accused against the forest warden. Your control is his ultimate and only guarantee. Imbued with a vague notion of your personal excellence, in poetic self-indulgence, you offer the parties in the case your individual qualities as a safeguard against your laws. I confess that I do not share this romantic conception of the forest owners. I do not at all believe that persons are guarantees against laws; on the contrary, I believe that laws must be a guarantee against persons. And will even the boldest imagination be able to envision men who, in the lofty work of legislation cannot for a moment rise above the narrow, practically base standpoint of self-seeking to the theoretical height of a universal and objective point of view, men who tremble even at the thought of future disadvantages and seize on anything solid to defend their interests? Can these men become philosophers in the face of real danger? But no one, not even the most exquisite legislator, is allowed to put himself above his own law. No one is authorized to decree a vote of confidence in himself when it entails consequences for third parties.

But you may judge from the following facts whether it is permissible for you even to demand that people should place special confidence in you. “He must oppose §87,” stated an urban deputy, “since its provisions would give rise to widespread and fruitless investigations, which would disturb personal freedom and commercial traffic. It is not permissible beforehand to regard everyone as a criminal and to assume a crime before having proof that it has been committed.”

Another urban deputy said that the paragraph ought to be deleted. The vexatious provision that “everyone has to prove where he obtained his wood,” with the result that everyone could be under suspicion of stealing and concealing wood, was a gross and injurious intrusion into the life of the citizen. The paragraph was adopted.

Truly, you suspect too much of human inconsistency if you expect them to proclaim as a maxim that distrust is to their detriment and confidence is to your advantage, and if you expect their confidence and distrust to see through the eyes of your private interest and feel through the heart of your private interest.

There is yet another argument against lifetime appointments, a reasoning so contradictory it is impossible to say whether it is formulated better to evoke contempt or ridicule. “*The free will of private persons* should not be restricted in so great a way, which is why only appointments that can be terminated should be allowed.”

Certainly, it is gratifying and unexpected news to hear that man possesses a free will that must not be restricted in any way. The oracles we have so far heard have resembled the ancient oracle at Dodona.[19] The wood was dividing them. Free will, however, does not have the quality of an estate. How are we to understand this sudden rebellious emergence of ideology, for as far as ideas are concerned, we have before us only followers of Napoleon?

The will of the forest owner requires freedom to deal with the infringer of forest regulations as it sees fit and in the way it finds most convenient and least costly. This will wants the state to hand over the villain to it to deal with at its discretion. It demands *plein pouvoir* [full powers]. It does not oppose the restriction of free will; it opposes the *manner* of this restriction, which is so restrictive that it affects both the infringer of forest regulations and also the owner of the wood. Does not this free will want to have numerous freedoms? Is it not a very free, an excellent, free will? And is it not unheard of in the nineteenth century to dare to restrict "in so great a way" [auf solche Weise so sehr] the free will of those private persons who promulgate public laws? It is, indeed, unheard of.

Even that obstinate reformer, free will, must join in following good arguments led by the sophistry of private interest. But this free will must have good manners; it must be a cautious, loyal free will, one that is able to arrange itself in such a way that its sphere coincides with the sphere of the arbitrary power of those same privileged private persons. Only once has there been mention of free will, and on this one occasion it appears in the shape of a squat private person who hurls blocks of wood at the spirit of rational will. Indeed, what need is there for this spirit where the will is chained to the most petty and narrow-minded interests like a galley slave to his rowing bench?

The climax of this whole argument is summarized in the following remark, which turns the relationship in question upside down: "While the royal forest and hunting wardens may be appointed for life, in the case of rural communities and private persons this evokes the most serious concerns."

As if the only concern was that private servants operate here in the place of state officials! As if life appointment was not aimed precisely against private persons, who are the ones that *evoke concerns*! *Rien n'est plus terrible que la logique dans l'absurdité,*[20] that is to say, nothing is more terrible than the logic of selfishness.

This logic, which turns the servant of the forest owner into a state authority, *turns the authority of the state into a servant of the forest owner.* The state structure, the purpose of the individual administrative authorities, everything must get out of control so that everything is degraded into an instrument of the forest owner and his interest operates as the soul governing the entire mechanism. All the organs of the state become ears, eyes, arms, legs with which the interest of the forest owner hears, observes, appraises, protects, grasps, and runs.

The commission proposed an addition to §62, a final sentence demanding that inability to pay be certified by the tax collector, the burgomaster, and two local officials of the community where the infringer of forest regulations lives. A deputy from the rural communities considered that to make use of the *tax collector* was contrary to existing legislation. Of course, no attention was paid to this contradiction.

For §20, the commission proposed:

> In the Rhine Province the authorized forest owner should be entitled to transfer convicted persons to the local authority to perform penal labor such that their working days will be calculated as part of the manual services on communal roads that the forest owner is obliged to render in the rural community, and accordingly subtracted from his obligation.

The objection was raised that

> burgomasters are not needed to serve as executives for individual members of the rural community, and that convict labor cannot be accepted as compensation for the services that have to be performed by paid day laborers or servants.

The spokesman commented:

> Even if it is a burden for the burgomaster to persuade reluctant and insubordinate prisoners convicted of infringing forest regulations to work, nevertheless it is one of the functions of these officials to induce disobedient and malicious persons in their charge to return to the path of duty, and is it not a *noble deed* to lead the convict away from the wrong road back to the right path? Who in the countryside has more means of doing this than the burgomasters?

> Meanwhile the Rogue so well had plied his art,
> Insisting on the blessings of repentance,

> He'd softened not a few of his Attendants;
> And especially the tender-hearted Hare
> From sympathetic tears could not forbear.[21]

The Provincial Assembly adopted the proposal.

Rheinische Zeitung, no. 305, November 1, 1842

The good burgomaster must undertake a burdensome task and perform a noble deed so that the forest owner can fulfill his duty to the community without expense to himself. [22] The forest owner could with equal right make use of the burgomaster as a chief cook or head waiter. Is it not a noble deed for the burgomaster to look after the kitchen or cellar of those in his charge? The convicted criminal is not in the charge of the burgomaster, but a charge of the prison superintendent. Does not the burgomaster lose the means and dignity of his position if he is converted from a representative of the community to an executor for individual members, if he is turned from a burgomaster into a taskmaster? Will not the other, free members of the community be insulted if their honest work for the general good is degraded to the level of penal labor in the service of particular individuals?

But it is superfluous to expose these sophistries. May the spokesman be so good as to tell us himself how worldly people judge humane phrases. He makes the *forest owner* harangue the humanizing *farm owner* in the following way:

> If some ears of corn are stolen from a landowner, the thief would say, "I have no bread, so I take a few ears of corn from the large amount you possess," just as the wood thief says, "I have no firewood, so I steal some wood." The landowner is protected by Article 444 of the Criminal Code, which punishes the taking of ears of corn with 2–5 years imprisonment. The forest owner has no such powerful protection.

This last envious exclamation of the forest owner contains a whole creed. Farm owners, why are you so magnanimous where my interests are concerned? Because *your* interests are already taken care of. So, let there be no illusions! Magnanimity either costs nothing or brings something in. Therefore, farm owner, do not deceive the forest owner! Therefore, forest owner, do not deceive the burgomaster!

This intermezzo alone would prove what little meaning "noble deeds" can have in our debate, if the whole debate did not prove that moral and humane reasons occur here merely as phrases. But interest is stingy even with phrases. It invents them only as is necessary, when it is to some considerable advantage. Then it becomes eloquent, its blood pumps faster, it is not sparing even with noble deeds that yield it profit at the expense of others, with flattering and sugarcoated words. Moreover, all of that is exploited only in order to convert the infringement of forest regulations into currency for the forest owner, to make the infringer of forest regulations into a lucrative source of income, to be able to invest the capital more conveniently—for the wood thief has become capital for the forest owner. It is not a question of misusing the burgomaster for the benefit of the infringer of forest regulations, but of misusing the burgomaster for the benefit of the forest owner. What a strange fate, what a surprising fact, that on the rare occasions when a problematic benefit for the infringer of forest regulations is given a passing mention, the forest owner is guaranteed an indisputable benefit!

The following is yet another example of these humane sentiments!

> *Spokesman*: "French law does not acknowledge the commutation of imprisonment into forest labor; he considers this commutation a wise and beneficial measure, for imprisonment does not always lead to reform but very often to corruption."

Previously, when innocent persons were turned into criminals, when a deputy remarked that by putting the pilferers of fallen wood in prison they were simply putting them into contact with inveterate thieves, prisons were said to be *good*. Suddenly correctional institutions have metamorphosed into corrupting institutions, because at this moment it is in the forest owner's interest that prisons corrupt. Reform of the criminal is now understood to mean *improvement of the percentage of profit* that it is the criminal's noble function to provide for the forest owner.

Interest has no memory; it thinks only of itself. The *one* thing about which it is concerned, itself, it never forgets. But it is not concerned with contradictions, for it never comes into contradiction with itself. It is a constant improviser, for it has no system, only *expedients* [Auskunftsmittel].

Whereas humane and rightful motives do nothing except

> *Ce qu'au bal nous autres sots humains,*
> *Nous appelons faire tapisserie,*[23]

expedients are the most active agents in the reasoning mechanism of private interest. Among these expedients, we note two that constantly recur in this debate and constitute the main categories, namely, *"good motives"* and *"harmful results."* We see sometimes the spokesman for the commission, sometimes another member of the Assembly, defending every ambiguous provision against hostile arrows of objections by means of the shield of shrewd, wise, and good motives. We see every conclusion drawn from the standpoint of right rejected by referring to its harmful or dangerous results. Let us examine for a moment these extensive expedients, these expedients par excellence, these expedients covering everything and a little more.

Interest knows the law from the perspective of the harmful results owing to its effects in the external world; it knows how to whitewash what is wrong by ascribing good motives to it, that is, by retreating into the internal world of thought. Law produces bad results in the external world among bad people, injustice has good motives in the breast of the honest man who decrees it; but both, the good motives and the harmful results, have in common the peculiar feature that they do not look at a thing in relation to itself, that they do not treat the law as an independent object, but direct attention away from the law either to the external world or to their own mind, that therefore they maneuver *behind the back of the law.*

What are harmful results? Our whole account has shown that they are not to be understood as harmful results for the state, the law, or the accused. Moreover, we should like to make quite clear in a few lines that they do not include harmful results for the *safety of citizens.*

We have already heard from members of the Assembly themselves that the provision by which "everyone has to prove where he obtained his wood" is a gross and injurious intrusion into the life of the citizen and makes every citizen the victim of vexatious harassment. Another provision declares everyone a thief in whose keeping stolen wood is found, even though a deputy stated: "This could be dangerous for many an honest man. Wood stolen by someone else might be thrown into the yard of an innocent man."

§66 condemns any citizen who buys a broom that is not issued under monopoly to a labor penitentiary [der Zuchthaus] from four weeks to two years. On this, an urban deputy commented as follows: "This paragraph threatens each and every citizen of the Elberfeld, Lennep, and Solingen districts with penal labor [Zuchthausstrafe]."

Finally, supervision and management of the game and forest police have been made not only a right but a duty of the *military,* even though Article 9 of the criminal code only recognizes officials under the supervision of state prosecutors (so they can be directly tracked by them), which is not the case with the military. This is a threat both to the independence of the courts and to the freedom and security of citizens.

Hence, instead of speaking about harmful results for the safety of citizens, their safety is treated as a *circumstance having harmful results.*

So, what are harmful results? Harmful is that which is harmful to the interests of the forest owner. If, therefore, the law does not result in the furtherance of his interests, its results are harmful. And in this respect interest is ingenious. Whereas previously it did not see what was obvious to the naked eye, it now sees even what is only visible through a microscope. The whole world is a thorn in the side of private interest, a world full of dangers, precisely because it is the world not of a single interest but of many interests. Private interest sees itself as the ultimate purpose of the world. Thus, if the law does not realize this ultimate purpose, it becomes inexpedient law. *Law that is harmful to private interests* is therefore *law with harmful results*.

Are *good motives* considered to be better than harmful results?

Interest does not think, it calculates. Motives are its figures. Motive is an incentive for abolishing the basis of law, and who can doubt that private interest will have many incentives for doing so? The goodness of a motive lies in the casual flexibility with which it can set aside the objective state of affairs and lull itself and others into the delusion that it is not necessary to keep one's mind on what is good; it is sufficient to have good thoughts while doing a bad thing.

Resuming the thread of our argument, we mention first of all an aside to the noble deeds recommended to the Herr Bürgermeister. "The commission proposed an amended version of §34 along the following lines: if the accused demands that the warden who drew up the charge be summoned, then he must also deposit with the forestry court *in advance* all the costs thereby incurred." The state and the court must not do anything gratis in the interests of the accused. They must demand payment in advance, which obviously in advance makes difficult any confrontation of the warden making the charge and the accused.

A noble deed! Just one single noble deed! My kingdom for a noble deed![24] But the only noble deed proposed is that which Herr Bürgermeister has to perform for the benefit of Herr Forest Owner. The burgomaster is the representative of noble deeds, their humanized expression, and the series of noble deeds is exhausted and ended forever with this burden, imposed with melancholy sacrifice on the burgomaster. If the burgomaster must do more than his duty for the good of the state and the moral benefit of the criminal, should not the forest owners, for the sake of the same good, demand *less* than their *private interest* requires?

One might think that the reply to this question had been given in part of the debate already dealt with, but that is a mistake. We come to the *penal provisions*.

> A deputy from the knightly estate still did not consider the forest owner inadequately compensated even if he received (over and above the simple replacement of the value) the amount of the fine imposed, which would often not be obtainable.
>
> An urban deputy remarked:
>
> The provisions of this paragraph (§15) could have the most serious consequences. The forest owner would receive *triple* compensation, namely: the value, then the four-, six-, or eightfold fine, and in addition a special sum as compensation for loss, which will often be assessed quite arbitrarily and will be the result of a fiction rather than of reality. In any case, it seemed necessary to him to direct that the special compensation in question should be claimed at once at the forestry court and awarded in the court's sentence. It was obvious from the nature of the case that proof of loss sustained should be supplied separately and could not be based merely on the warden's report.

Opposing this, the speaker and another member explained how the *additional value* mentioned here could arise in various cases indicated by them. The paragraph was adopted.

Crime becomes a lottery in which the forest owner, if he is lucky, can even win a prize. There can be additional value, but the forest owner, who already receives the simple value, can also make a profitable business out of the four-, six-, or eightfold fine. But if, besides the simple value, he receives special compensation for loss, the four-, six-, or eightfold fine is also sheer profit. If a member of the knightly estate thinks the money accruing as a fine is an inadequate guarantee because it would often not be obtainable, it would certainly not become more obtainable by the value and the compensation for loss having to be recovered as well. We shall see presently how this difficulty of receiving money from the accused is overcome.

Could the forest owner have any better insurance for his wood than what has happened here, whereby crime has been turned into a source of income? Like a skilled general he converts the attack against him into an infallible opportunity for a profitable victory, because even the additional value of the wood, an economic fantasy, is turned into a substance by theft. The forest owner must be guaranteed not only his wood, but also his wood business, while the convenient homage he pays to his business manager, the state, consists in not paying for its services. It is a remarkable idea to turn the punishment of crime from a victory of the law over attacks on it into a victory of selfishness over attacks on selfishness.

In particular, however, we draw our readers' attention to the provision of §14, which compels us to abandon the customary idea that *leges barbarorum* are laws of barbaric peoples. *Punishment* as such, the restoration of the law, which must certainly be distinguished from restitution of the value and compensation for loss, the restoration of private property, is transformed from *a public punishment* into *a private compensation,* the fines going not to the state treasury, but to the private coffers of the forest owner.

An urban deputy stated: "This is contrary to the dignity of the state and the principles of correct criminal jurisprudence," but a deputy from the knightly estate appealed to the Assembly's sense of right and fairness to protect the rights of the forest owner, that is to say, he appealed to a *special* sense of right and fairness.

Barbaric peoples order the payment of definite monetary

compensation (atonement) to the injured person for a definite crime. The concept of public punishment arose only in opposition to this view, which sees in crime only a violation to the individual, but the people and the theory have yet to be invented that are so complacent as to allow an individual to claim for himself both the private punishment and that imposed by the state.

A complete quid pro quo must have seduced the Assembly. The lawgiving forest owner confused for a moment his two roles, that of legislator and that of forest owner. In one case, as a forest owner he made the thief pay him for the wood. And in the other, as a legislator he made the thief pay him for the thief's *criminal frame of mind,* and it happened quite by chance that in both cases it was the forest owner who was paid. So, we are no longer faced by the simple *droit du seigneur.*[25] We have passed through the era of public law to the era of double patrimonial right, exponential patrimonial right. Patrimonial property owners have taken advantage of the progress of time, which is the refutation of their demands, in order to usurp both the private punishment of the barbaric worldview and the public punishment typical of the modern one.

Owing to the refunding of the value and even special compensation for loss, the relation between the wood thief and the forest owner has ceased to exist, for the infringement of forest regulations has been completely abolished. Both thief and property owner have returned to their former state in its entirety. The forest owner has suffered by the theft of wood only insofar as the wood has suffered, but not insofar as the law has been violated. Only the sensuously perceptible aspect of the crime affects him, but the criminal nature of the act does not consist in the attack on the wood as a material object, but in the attack on the wood as part of the state system, an attack on the right to property as such, the realization of a wrongful frame of mind. Does the forest owner have private claims to the legal disposition [Gesinnung] of the theft? And what is the multiplication of the punishment for a repetition of the offense except a punishment for a criminal disposition? Or can the forest owner make private demands where he has no private claims? Was the forest owner the state, prior to the theft of wood? He was not, but he becomes it after the theft. The wood possesses the remarkable character such that as soon as it is stolen it secures for its owner state qualities it did not previously possess. The forest owner can only get back what has been taken from him. If the state is given back to him—and given back to him by according him not simply a private right, but the state's right over the lawbreaker—then he must have been robbed of the state, the state must have been his private property. Therefore, the wood thief, like a second Saint Christopher, carried the state itself on his back in the form of the stolen wood.

Public punishment is the adjustment of crime to the reason of state; it is therefore a right of the state, but it is a right that the state can no more cede to private persons than one person can relinquish his conscience to another. Every right of the state in relation to the criminal is at the same time a right of the criminal in relation to the state. No interposing of intermediate links can convert the relation of a criminal to the state into a relation between him and private persons. Even if one wanted to permit the state to give up its rights, that is, to commit suicide, such an abandonment of its obligations would be not merely negligence, but a crime.

It is therefore as impossible for the forest owner to obtain from the state a private right to public punishment as it is for him to have any conceivable right, in and for himself, to impose public punishment. If, in the absence of a rightful claim to do so, I make the criminal act of a third person an independent source of income for myself, do I not thus become his accomplice? Or am I less so his accomplice because punishment falls to him, while the fruits of the crime fall to me? Guilt is not mitigated if a private person abuses his status as a legislator to arrogate to himself rights belonging to the state because of a crime committed by a third person. Embezzling of public, state funds is a crime against the state. Is not money from fines public money belonging to the state?

The wood thief has robbed the forest owner of wood, but the

forest owner has used the wood thief to steal the *state itself*. How literally true this is can be seen from §19, the provisions of which do not stop at imposing a fine but also lay claim to the *body and life* of the accused. According to §19, the infringer of forest regulations is handed over completely to the forest owner, for whom he has to perform *forest labor,* which, according to an urban deputy, "could lead to great inconvenience. He wished merely to call attention to the danger of this procedure in the case of persons of the other sex."

> A deputy from the knightly estate gave the following eternally memorable reply: "While it is as necessary as it is expedient to discuss in advance the principles of the law when discussing a bill, it should also be noted that, once this has been done, there can be no going back to them in discussing each separate paragraph."

After this, the paragraph was adopted *without opposition*.

Be clever enough to start out from bad principles, and you cannot fail to be rightfully entitled to the bad consequences. You might think, of course, that the worthlessness of the principle would be revealed in the abnormity of its consequences, but if you knew the world you would realize that, once they have set something in place, the clever take full advantage of every consequence following from it. We are only surprised that the forest owner is not allowed to heat his stove with the wood thieves. Because it is a question not of right, but of the principles that the Provincial Assembly has chosen to take as its starting point, there is not the slightest bump in the road to the realization of this consequence.

In direct contradiction to the dogma enunciated above, a brief retrospective glance teaches us how necessary it would have been to discuss the principles afresh in respect of each paragraph; how, by voting on paragraphs that were apparently unconnected and very remote from one another, one provision after another was surreptitiously *slipped through*; and how, once the first has been put through in this way, subsequent provisions could be accepted without even the *semblance* of the condition required for the first.

Rheinische Zeitung, no. 307, November 3, 1842

When in connection with §4 the question arose of entrusting appraisal of value to the warden making the charge, an urban deputy remarked: "If the proposal that fines should be paid into the state treasury is not approved, the provision under discussion will be doubly dangerous."[26]

It is clear that the forest warden will not have the same motive for overestimating if his appraisal is made for the state and not for his employer. Discussion of this point was commonly avoided, the impression being given that §14, which awards the money from the fine to the forest owner, could be rejected. §4 was adopted. After voting ten paragraphs, the Assembly arrived at §14, by which §4 was given an altered and dangerous meaning. But this connection was totally ignored; §14 was adopted, providing for fines to be paid into the private accounts of the forest owners. The main reason (indeed the only one) is the interest of the forest owner, which is insufficiently compensated by the reimbursement of the simple value. But in §15 it has been forgotten that it was voted that the fine should be paid to the forest owner and it is decreed that he should receive, besides the simple value, a special compensation for loss, because it was thought proper that he should have an additional value, as if he had not already received such an addition thanks to the fines flowing into his accounts. It has even been noted that the fines could not always be obtainable from the accused. Thus, the *impression was given* that only in regard to the money was it intended to take the place of the state, but in §19 the mask is discarded and a claim advanced not only for the money, but for the criminal himself, not only for the man's wallet, but for himself.

At this point the method of the deception emerges sharply

and frankly, indeed in self-conscious clarity, for there is no longer any hesitation to proclaim it as a principle.

The right to replacement of the simple value and compensation for loss obviously gave the forest owner only a *private claim* against the wood thief, for the implementation of which the civil courts were available. If the wood thief cannot pay, the forest owner is in the position of any private person faced with an insolvent debtor, and, of course, that does not give him any right to compulsory labor, corvée services, or, in short, *temporary serfdom* of the debtor. What gives the forest owner this claim? The *fine*. As we have seen, by appropriating the fine for himself, the forest owner claims not only his private right, but also the *state's right* to the wood thief, and so puts himself in the place of the state. In awarding the fine to himself, however, the forest owner has cleverly concealed that he has accorded himself the right of *punishment itself*. Whereas previously he spoke of the *fine* simply as a sum of *money*, he now refers to it as a *punishment* and triumphantly admits that by means of the fine he has converted a public right into private property. Instead of recoiling in horror before this consequence, which is as criminal as it is revolting, people accept it precisely because it is a consequence. Common sense may maintain that it is contrary to our concept of right, to every kind of right, to hand over one citizen to another as a temporary serf, but shrugging their shoulders, people declare that the principle has been discussed, although there has been neither principle nor discussion. In this way, by means of the fine, the forest owner surreptitiously obtains control over the *person of the wood thief*. Only §19 reveals the double meaning of §14.

Thus, we see that §4 should have been impossible because of §14, §14 because of §15, §15 because of §19, and §19 itself is simply impossible and should have made impossible the entire principle of the punishment, precisely because in it all the depravity of this principle is revealed.

The principle of *divide et impera*[27] could not be more skillfully deployed. In considering one paragraph, no attention is paid to the next, and when the turn of that one comes, the preceding one is forgotten. One paragraph has already been discussed, the other has not yet been discussed, so for opposite reasons both of them are raised to a position above all discussion. But the accepted principle is "the sense of right and fairness in protecting the interests of the forest owner," which is directly opposed to the sense of right and fairness in protecting the interests of those whose property consists of life, freedom, humanity, and citizenship of the state—those who own nothing but themselves.

We have, however, reached a point where the forest owner, in exchange for his piece of wood, receives what was once a human being.

> *Shylock:* Most learned judge!—A sentence! come, prepare!
> *Portia:* Tarry a little; there is something else.
> This bond doth give thee here no jot of blood,—
> The words expressly are 'a pound of flesh':
> Take then thy bond, take thou thy pound of flesh;
> But, in the cutting it, if thou dost shed
> One drop of Christian blood, thy lands and goods
> Are, by the laws of Venice, confiscate
> Unto the state of Venice.
> *Gratiano:* O upright judge!—Mark, Jew:—O learned judge!
> *Shylock:* Is that the law?
> *Portia:* Thyself shalt see the act.[28]

You, too, should see the act!

How do you explain your claim to be able to convert the wood thief into a serf? The fine. We have shown that you have no right to the fines. Leaving this out of account, what is your basic principle? That the interests of the forest owner shall be secured even if this results in destroying the world of law and freedom. You are unshakably determined that *in some way or other* the wood thief must *compensate* you for the *loss* of your *wood.* This firm wooden foundation of your argument is so rotten that a single gust of sound reasoning is sufficient to shatter it into a thousand fragments.

The state can and must say: I guarantee right against all contingencies. Right alone is immortal in me, and therefore I prove to you the mortality of crime by revoking it. But the state cannot and must not say: a private interest, a particular existence of property, a wooded plot of land, a tree, a chip of wood (and compared to the state the greatest tree is hardly more than a chip of wood) is guaranteed against all contingencies, is immortal. The state cannot go against the nature of things; it cannot make the finite proof against the conditions of the finite, against chance. Just as your property cannot be guaranteed by the state against all contingencies *before* a crime, so also a crime cannot convert this uncertain nature of your property into its opposite. Of course, the state will safeguard your private interests insofar as these can be safeguarded by rational laws and rational measures of prevention, but the state cannot concede to your private demand in respect of the criminal any other right than the right of private demands, the protection given by civil jurisdiction. If you cannot obtain any compensation from the criminal in this way owing to his lack of means, the only consequence is that *all legal means* to secure compensation have come to an end. The world will not come unhinged on that account, nor will the state forsake the sunlit path of justice, but you will have experienced the transience of all earthly things, an experience that will hardly appear to your dignified religiosity as a piquant novelty, as more astonishing than storms, conflagrations, or fevers. If, however, the state wanted to make the criminal your temporary serf, it would sacrifice the immortality of the law to your finite private interests. It would thereby prove to the criminal the mortality of the law, whereas by punishment it ought to prove to him its immortality.

When, during the reign of King Philip, Antwerp could easily have kept the Spaniards at bay by flooding its territory, the butchers' guild would not agree to this because they had fat oxen in the pastures.[29] You demand that the state should abandon its spiritual territory in order to avenge your pieces of wood.

There are still some ancillary provisions of §16 to be discussed.

An urban deputy notes: "Under current legislation, eight days' imprisonment would be equivalent to a fine of five talers. There is no sufficient reason for departing from this." (Namely, for making it fourteen days instead of eight.) The commission proposed the following addition to the same paragraph: "that in no case a prison sentence should last less than twenty-four hours." When someone suggested that this minimum was too great, a deputy from the knightly estate retorted: "The French forestry law does not have any punishment of less than three days." In the same breath as it opposed the provision of the French law by making fourteen days' imprisonment instead of eight the equivalent of a fine of five talers, the Assembly, out of devotion to the French law, opposed the three days being altered to twenty-four hours.

The above-mentioned urban deputy remarked further:

> It would be very severe at least to impose fourteen days' imprisonment as an equivalent for a fine of five talers for wood theft, which after all cannot be regarded as a crime deserving heavy punishment. The result would be that the average person, who has the means to buy his freedom, would suffer simple punishment whereas the punishment of a poor person would be doubled.

A deputy from the knightly estate mentioned that in the neighborhood of Cleve many wood thefts took place merely in order to secure shelter and food in the detention center. Does this deputy from the knightly estate not prove precisely what he wants to refute, namely, that people are driven to steal wood by the sheer necessity of saving themselves from starvation and homelessness? Is this terrible need an aggravating circumstance?

The previously mentioned *urban deputy* said also: "The cut in prison rations, which has already been condemned, must be regarded as too severe and, especially in the case of *penal labor,* quite impracticable." A number of deputies denounced the reduction of food to *bread* and *water* as too severe. But a deputy from a rural community remarked that in the Trier district the reduction in rations had already been introduced and had proved to be very *effective*.

Why did the honorable speaker find that the beneficial effect in Trier was owing precisely to bread and water and not, perhaps, to the *intensification of religious sentiment*, about which the Assembly was able to speak so much and so movingly? Who could have dreamed at that time that bread and water were the true means of salvation? During certain debates one could believe that the English Holy Parliament[30] had been revived. And now? Instead of prayer and trust and song, we have bread and water, prison and labor in the forest! How generously the Assembly is paraded with words in order to procure the Rhinelanders a seat in heaven! How lavish is it with words too in order that a whole class of Rhinelanders should be fed on bread and water and driven with whips to labor in the forest—an idea that a Dutch plantation owner would hardly dare to entertain in regard to his Negroes. What does all this prove? That it is easy to be holy if you don't want to be human. That is the way in which the following passage can be understood: "A member of the Assembly considered the provision in §23 *inhuman*; nevertheless, it was adopted." Apart from its *inhumanity*, nothing more was reported about this paragraph.

Our whole account has shown how the Assembly degrades the executive power, the administrative authorities, the existence of the accused, the idea of the state, crime itself, and punishment as well, down to the *material means of private interest*. It will be consistently found, therefore, that the *verdict of the court* is also treated as a mere means, and the *legal validity* of the sentence as a superfluous verbosity.

> In §6 the commission proposed to delete the words *"legally binding"* [rechtskräftig] because, in cases of judgment by default, their adoption would give the wood thief a ready means of avoiding an increased punishment for a repetition of the offense. On the other hand, however, many deputies protested against this, declaring that it was necessary to oppose the commission's proposed deletion of the

expression *"legally binding judgment"* [rechtskräftiges Urteil] in §6 of the draft. The description of judgments included in this paragraph was certainly not made without judicial consideration. If, however, every first sentence pronounced by the judge was sufficient grounds for imposing a severer punishment later, then, of course, the intention of punishing repeated offenders more severely would be more easily and frequently achieved. It had to be considered, however, whether one was willing to sacrifice in this way an *essential legal principle* to the *interests of forest protection* stressed by the spokesman. One could not agree that the violation of an indisputable basic principle of judicial procedure could give such a result to a sentence that was still without legal validity. Another urban deputy also called for the rejection of the commission's amendment. He said the amendment violated the provisions of the criminal law by which there could be no increase of punishment until the first punishment had been established by a legally valid sentence. The spokesman for the commission retorted: "The *whole forms an exceptional law,* and therefore also an *exceptional provision,* such as has been proposed, is permissible in it." The commission's proposal to delete the words "legally valid" was *approved.*

The sentence exists merely to identify recidivism. The judicial forms seem to the greedy restlessness of private interest to be cumbersome and superfluous obstacles of a pedantic legal etiquette. The trial is just a safe way to put the opponent in prison, mere preparation for execution, and if the trial seeks to be more than that it has to be silenced. The anxiety of self-interest peeks out, calculates and combines in the most accurate manner how the enemy could exploit the legal terrain on which, as a necessary evil, he has to be encountered, and where the most cautious countermaneuvers are undertaken. The law itself is encountered here as an obstacle to the unbridled pursuit of private interest, and is treated accordingly. You haggle and bargain with it to secure the negation of a basic principle here and there; you appease it with the most suppliant references to the right of private interest; you slap it on the shoulder and whisper in its ear: these are exceptions and there are no rules without an exception. You try to compensate for the slippery slope of consciousness by treating the law as a guarantee of the accused and as an independent object, all the while permitting it meticulous terrorism in relation to the enemy.[31] The interest of the law is allowed to speak insofar as it is the law of private interest, but it has to be silent as soon as it comes into conflict with this holy of holies.

The forest owner, who himself *punishes,* is so consistent that he himself also *judges,* for he obviously acts as a judge by declaring a sentence legally binding although it has no legal validity. What kind of foolish, impractical illusion is a nonpartisan judge at all when the legislature itself is bias? What is a disinterested judgment when the law itself is self-interested? The judge can only formulate the self-interest of the law puritanically, only ruthlessly apply it. Impartiality is then only the form, not the content, of the sentence. The content has been anticipated by the law. If the trial is nothing but an empty form, then such a trivial formality has no independent value. According to this view, Chinese law would become French law if it was forced into the French procedure, but *substantive law* has its own *necessary, native trial form.* Just as the rod necessarily figures in Chinese law, and just as torture has a place in the medieval criminal code as a form of trial, so the public, free trial, in accordance with its own nature, necessarily has a public content dictated by freedom and not by private interest. Court trial and the law are no more indifferent to each other than, for instance, the forms of plants are indifferent to the plants themselves, and the forms of animals to their flesh and blood. There must be a *single* spirit animating the trial and the law, for the trial is only the *form of life of the law,* the manifestation of its inner life.

The pirates of Tidong break the arms and legs of their prisoners to ensure control over them.[32] To ensure control over wood thieves, the Provincial Assembly has not only broken the arms and legs of the law, but has even pierced its heart. We consider its merit in regard to reestablishing some categories of our trial procedure as absolutely nil; on the contrary, we must acknowledge the frankness and consistency with which it gives unfree form to unfree content. If private interest, which cannot bear the light of publicity, is introduced materially into our law, then one also gives it here its appropriate form, that of secret procedure so that at least no dangerous, complacent illusions will be evoked and entertained. We consider that at the present moment it is the duty of all Rhinelanders, and especially of Rhineland jurists, to devote their main attention to the *content of the law,* so that we should not be left in the end with only an empty mask. The form is of no value if it is not the form of the content.

The commission's proposal that we have just examined and the Assembly's vote approving it are the climax to the whole debate, for here the Assembly itself becomes conscious of the *conflict between the interest of forest protection and the principles of law,* principles endorsed by our own laws. The Assembly therefore put it to the vote whether the principles of law should be sacrificed to the interest of forest protection or whether this interest should be sacrificed to the principles of law, and *interest overruled law.* It was even realized that the whole law was an *exception to the law,* and therefore the conclusion was drawn that *every* exceptional provision it contained was permissible. The Assembly confined itself to drawing consequences that the legislator had neglected. Wherever the legislator had forgotten that it was a question of an exception to the law, and not the law itself, i.e., wherever he put forward the legal point of view, our Assembly by its activity intervened with confident tactfulness to correct and supplement him, and to make private interest lay down the law to the law, where the law had laid down the law to private interest.

The Provincial Assembly has thus *completely fulfilled its mission.*[33] In accordance with its *function,* it represented a definite *particular interest* and treated it as the ultimate end. That in doing so it trampled the law under foot is a *simple consequence of its task,* for interest by its very nature is blind, excessive, one-sided; in short, it is lawless natural instinct, and can lawlessness lay down laws? Private interest is no more made capable of legislating by being installed on the throne of the legislator than a mute is made capable of speech by being given an enormous megaphone [ein Sprachrohr].

We have only reluctantly followed this tedious and mindless debate, but we considered it our duty to show by means of an example what is to be expected from an *Assembly of the Estates of particular interests* if it were ever seriously called upon to legislate.

We repeat once again: our estates have fulfilled their function as such, but far be it for us to desire to justify them on that account. In them, the Rhinelander ought to have been victorious over the estate, the human being ought to have been victorious over the forest owner. They themselves are legally entrusted not only with the representation of particular interests but also with the representation of the interests of the province, and however contradictory these two tasks may be, in case of conflict one should not pause for a moment to sacrifice the representation of particular interest to representation of the interests of the province. The sense of right and legality is the *most important provincial characteristic* of the Rhinelander; but it goes without saying that a particular interest, caring no more for the province than it does for the Fatherland, has also no concern for local spirit, any more than for the general spirit. In direct contradiction to those fantasy writers whose ideal romanticism professes to find immeasurable depths of feeling, the most fruitful source of individual and specific forms of morality in the representation of private interests, such representation on the contrary abolishes all natural and spiritual distinctions by crowning in their place the immoral, irrational, and soulless abstraction of a particular material object and a particular consciousness that is slavishly subordinated to this object.

Wood remains wood in Siberia just as in France; forest owners remain forest owners in Kamchatka as in the Rhine Province. Thus, if wood and its owners as such make laws, these laws will differ from one another only by the place of origin and the language in which they are written. This *abject materialism,* this sin against the holy spirit of the people and humanity, is an immediate consequence of the doctrine that the *Preussische Staats-Zeitung* preaches to the legislator, namely, that in connection with the law concerning wood he should think only of wood and forest and should solve each material problem in a *nonpolitical way,* that is, without connection to the general reason and morality of the state.

The *savages of Cuba* regarded gold as a *fetish of the Spaniards.* They celebrated a feast in its honor, sang in a circle around it, and then threw it into the sea. If the Cuban savages had been present at the sitting of the Rhine Province Assembly, would they not have regarded wood as the *Rhinelanders' fetish*? But a subsequent sitting would have taught them that the worship of animals is connected with this fetishism, and they would have thrown *hares* into the sea in order to save the *human beings.*[34]

Selected Works by Daniel Bensaïd

Cataloging all of Bensaïd's publications and writings is unusually difficult because he was so prolific across a range of genres. In particular, he was adept at producing short topical pieces on areas of contemporary concern, essays that were then published as stand-alone writings. By all accounts, he was a master orator and pamphleteer. A list of his most important works in French must include the following.

Walter Benjamin: sentinelle messianique (Paris: Plon, 1990)

Jeanne de guerre lasse (Paris: Gallimard, 1991)

La discordance des temps: essais sur les crises, les classes, l'histoire (Paris: Éditions de la Passion, 1995)

Marx l'intempestif: grandeurs et misères d'une aventure critique (Paris: Fayard, 1995).

Le pari mélancolique (Paris: Fayard, 1997)

Contes et légendes de la guerre éthique (Paris: Éditions Textuel, 1999)

Éloge de la résistance à l'air du temps (Paris: Éditions Textuel, 1999)

Qui est le juge? (Paris: Fayard, 1999)

Le sourire du spectre (Paris: Michalon, 2000)

Karl Marx, les hieroglyphs de la modernité (Paris: Éditions Textuel, 2001)

Les irréductibles (Paris: Éditions Textuel, 2001)

Les Trotskismes (Paris: Presses universitaires de France [PUF], 2002)

Une lente impatience (Paris: Stock, 2004)

Fragments mécréants: mythes identitaires et république imaginaire (Paris: Édition Lignes, 2005)

Sur la question juive (Paris: La fabrique, 2006)

Éloge de la politique profane (Paris: Albin Michel, 2007)

Les Dépossédés (Paris: La fabrique, 2007)

Prenons parti! (avec Olivier Besancenot) (Paris: Mille et une nuits, 2009)

Une radicalité joyeusement mélancolique (Paris: Éditions Textuel, 2010)

Writings by Bensaïd have been translated into many languages, including Basque, German, Greek, Hungarian, Italian, Japanese, Korean, Portuguese, Russian, Spanish, and Turkish. The best-known English translations are:

A Marx for Our Times: Adventures and Misadventures of a Critique (London: Verso, 2002), translation of *Marx l'intempestif: grandeurs et misères d'une aventure critique*

"Permanent Scandal," in *Democracy in What State?* (New York: Columbia University Press, 2012), translation of *Démocratie, dans quel état?* (Paris: La fabrique, 2009)

An Impatient Life: A Memoir (London: Verso, 2014), translation of *Une lente impatience*

Strategies of Resistance: "Who Are the Trotskyists?" (London: Resistance Books, 2013), translation of *Les Trotskismes* (Paris: PUF, 2002)

Essays in translation have also been included in *Take the Power to Change the World: Globalisation and the Debate on Power* (Iire Notebook for Study and Research, 2007); *The Long March of the Trotskyists' Contributions to the History of the Fourth International,* by Pierre Frank and Daniel Bensaïd (2010); and *Unity and Strategy: Ideas for Revolution. The Transitional Program for Socialist Revolution and Other Writings,* by Leon Trotsky and Daniel Bensaïd (2015).

A special issue of *Historical Materialism* is devoted to Bensaïd and his legacy; it includes two of his essays in English translation for the first time: *Historical Materialism* 24, no. 4 (2016).

Notes

Crisis and Kleptocracy

1. Klaus Deininger and Derek Byerlee, *Rising Global Interest in Farmland: Can It Yield Sustainable and Equitable Benefits?* (Washington, D.C.: World Bank, 2010), xiv.
2. Saturnino Borras, Ruth Hall, Ian Scoones, Ben White, and Wendy Wolford, "Towards a Better Understanding of Global Land Grabbing: An Editorial Introduction," *Journal of Peasant Studies* 38 (2011): 209–16, 209. For an insightful exploration of these issues, see Onur Ulas Ince, "Primitive Accumulation, New Enclosures, and Global Land Grabs: A Theoretical Intervention," *Rural Sociology* 79.1 (2014): 104–31.
3. For a sample of historical work on the English commons, see R. H. Tawney, *The Agrarian Problem in the Sixteenth Century* (London: Longmans, 1912); J. A. Yelling, *Common Field and Enclosure in England, 1450–1850* (London: Macmillan, 1977); J. M. Neeson, *Commoners: Common Right, Enclosure and Social Change in England, 1700–1820* (Cambridge: Cambridge University Press, 1993); Peter Linebaugh, *Stop, Thief! The Commons, Enclosures, and Resistance* (Oakland, Calif.: PM Press, 2014). The Midnight Notes Collective has had a shifting membership over the years but has included prominent intellectuals such as George Caffentzis, Peter Linebaugh, and Silvia Federici. Some representative publications include *Strange Victories* (1979), *No Future Notes* (1979), *The Work/Energy Crisis and the Apocalypse* (1980) and, most pertinently, *The New Enclosures* (1990). For a survey and links to online publications, see https://godsandradicals.org/2015/08/21/revolution-at-the-witching-hour/.
4. Biographical and historical material on this period of Marx's life is gleaned from Gareth Stedman Jones, *Karl Marx: Greatness and Illusion* (New York: Allen Lane, 2016), chapter 4, especially 104–21; Sven-Eric Liedman, *A World to Win: The Life and Works of Karl Marx* (New York: Verso, 2018), especially 78–105; David McLellan, *Karl Marx: A Biography* (London: Palgrave Macmillan, 1973), chapter 1, especially Part III, 36–49; Franz Mehring, *Karl Marx: The Story of His Life* (New York: Covici Friede Publishers, 1935), 58–85; Jonathan Sperber, *Karl Marx: A Nineteenth-Century Life* (New York: Liveright Publishing, 2013), chapter 3, 71–107; Francis Whelen, *Karl Marx: A Life* (New York: W. W. Norton, 1999), chapter 2, especially 34–48.

5. Marx returned to these themes in the articles of May 5, 8, 10, 12, 15, and 19, 1842. He likewise makes repeated reference to the concern with censorship, and his eventual battles to keep the *Rheinische Zeitung* open, in his correspondence from that period. See Karl Marx, *The Letters of Karl Marx, Selected and Translated with Explanatory Notes and an Introduction by Saul K. Padover* (Englewood Cliffs, N.J.: Prentice-Hall, 1979), 16–23.
6. For Marx's evaluation of Rutenberg, see, for instance, his letter to Arnold Ruge from November 30, 1842. There, he complains that the "monstrous stupidity" of the Prussian censors had labeled Rutenberg a danger, even though "he was dangerous to nobody except the *Rheinische Zeitung* and himself" (ibid., 20).
7. Jones, *Karl Marx*, 108.
8. For some of the commentary in English, see Heinz Lubasz, "Marx's Initial Problematic: The Problem of Poverty," *Political Studies* 24.1 (March 1976): 24–42; Arthur McGovern, "Marx's First Political Writings: The *Rheinische Zeitung* 1842–43," in F. J. Adelmann, ed., *Demythologising Marxism* (The Hague: Martinus Nijhoff, 1969); David McLellan, *Marx before Marxism* (New York: Harper & Row, 1970), chapter 4; Erica Sherover-Marcuse, *Emancipation and Consciousness: Dogmatic and Dialectical Perspectives in the Early Marx* (Oxford and New York: Blackwell, 1986), chapter 1.
9. Karl Marx, "Preface," in *A Contribution to the Critique of Political Economy*, trans. N. J. Stone (Chicago: Charles H. Kerr & Co., 1911), 10.
10. Quoted in McLellan, *Karl Marx*, 45–46.
11. "That crises are one of the most powerful levers of political upheaval has already been pointed out in the *Communist Manifesto* and was expounded in the *Neue Rheinische Zeitung* up to and including 1848" (Friedrich Engels, "Letter to Bernstein," January 25, 1882, in *Marx and Engels Collected Works*, vol. 46 (Moscow: Progress Publishers, 1965).
12. "Labour is, first of all, a process between man and nature, a process by which man, through his own actions, mediates, regulates and controls the metabolism between himself and nature" (Karl Marx, *Capital*, vol. 1 [New York: Penguin, 1990], 283).
13. Karl Marx, "On the Jewish Question," in Robert Tucker, ed., *The Marx-Engels Reader*, 2d ed. (New York and London: W. W. Norton, 1978), 33.
14. Daniel Bensaïd, Part I, "'Rural Pauperism' and 'Forest Malfeasance.'"
15. Ralph Miliband, *The State in Capitalist Society* (1969) was reviewed by Nicos Poulantzas in *New Left Review*, which sparked a debate across the channel between the two major figures of Marxist theory. Poulantzas would later publish his own "structuralist" account in *L'État, le pouvoir, le socialisme* (1978). The debate was republished in Robin Blackburn, ed., *Ideology in Social Science: Readings in Critical Social Theory* (New York: Pantheon, 1972), chapter 11, 238–62.
16. The most systematic analysis of the Rhineland articles in French (cited extensively by Bensaïd) is by Pierre Lascoumes and Hartwig Zander in *Marx, du «vol de bois» à la critique du droit* (Paris: PUF, 1982). For other useful works, see Paul Sereni, *Marx: La personne et la chose* (Paris: L'Harmattan, 2007), and Mikhail Xifaras, "Marx, justice et jurisprudence: une lecture

des 'Vols de bois,'" *Revue française d'histoire des idées politiques,* no. 15 (2002): 63–112.

17. For an examination of similar themes relative to finance capital today, see Ivan Ascher, *The Portfolio Society: On the Capitalist Mode of Prediction* (Cambridge: Zone/MIT Press, 2016).
18. See Guy Standing, *The Precariate: A New Dangerous Class* (New York: Bloomsbury, 2011) and, e.g., Achille Mbembe, *On the Postcolony* (Berkeley: University of California Press, 2001) and *Critique of Black Reason* (Durham, N.C.: Duke University Press, 2017).
19. There has been some discussion of "the multitude" as a potential twenty-first-century inheritor to the proletariat. However, it seems to me that this remains a vague promise largely lacking an account of the political-economic conditions that could effectively knit these groups together such that they might work effectively as a revolutionary force.
20. Robert Nichols, *Theft Is Property! Dispossession and Critical Theory* (Durham, N.C.: Duke University Press, 2020).
21. Daniel Bensaïd, *An Impatient Life,* (London: Verso, 2013), 152.
22. Daniel Bensaïd, *La discordance des temps: essais sur les crises, les classes, l'histoire* (Paris: Éditions de la Passion, 1995). An English translation of one essay from this collection can be found as Daniel Bensaïd, "The Time of Crises (and Cherries)," *Historical Materialism* 24.4 (2016): 9–35. As the editors of that special edition (Cinzia Arruzza and Patrick King) note, the title is a pun (*crises* rhymes with *cerises* in French) that references a song associated with the Paris Commune ("Le Temps des cerises"). See Cinzia Arruzza and Patrick King, "Introduction," *Historical Materialism* 24.4 (2016): 3–8.
23. Walter Benjamin, "Critique of Violence," in *Reflections: Essays, Aphorisms, and Autobiographical Writings,* edited and introduced by Peter Demetz (New York: Schocken, 1978), 277–300.
24. For his writings on these themes, see especially Bensaïd, *La discordance des temps.*
25. Enzo Traverso, "Synchronic Times: Walter Benjamin and Daniel Bensaïd," in *Left-Wing Melancholia: Marxism, History, and Memory* (New York: Columbia University Press, 2010), 229.
26. Daniel Bensaïd, *Walter Benjamin: sentinelle messianique, à la gauche du possible* (Paris: Les Prairies ordinaires, 2010).
27. For a collection of critical essays that treat Bensaïd in this "untimely" manner, see François Sabado, ed., *Daniel Bensaïd, l'intempestif* (Paris: La Découverte, 2012).
28. For some popular and academic uses of "kleptocracy" as a framework of analysis, see Daron Acemoglu, Thierry Verdier, and James Robinson, "Kleptocracy and Divide-and-Rule: A Mode of Personal Rule," *Journal of the European Economic Association* 2.2–3 (April–May 2004): 162–92; Franklin Foer, "Russian-Style Kleptocracy Is Infiltrating American," *Atlantic* (March 2019); National Endowment for Democracy, "The Big Question: What Is the Relationship between Kleoptocracy and Authoritarianism?" (https://www.ned.org/the-big-question-what-is-the-relationship-between-kleptocracy-and-authoritarianism/), published November 16, 2017.

29. In this way, the discussion here dovetails with recent work on neoliberal rationality, particularly that of Wendy Brown. See Wendy Brown, *Undoing the Demos: Neoliberalism's Stealth Revolution* (New York: Zone Books, 2015).
30. Bensaïd, *An Impatient Life,* 12.
31. Ibid., 65.
32. Ideologically, the JCR was informed by the Trotskyism of, for instance, Pierre Frank and Ernest Mandel. Its main rival was, for many years, the Organisation Communiste Internationaliste, which was more easily co-opted into Mitterrand's vision for the Socialist Party (hence the eventual success of Lionel Jospin).
33. Bensaïd, *An Impatient Life,* 46.
34. Ibid., 49.
35. Ibid., 76.
36. Kristin Ross, *May '68 and Its Afterlives* (Chicago: University of Chicago Press, 2002).
37. Bensaïd, *An Impatient Life,* 101.
38. See Bill Marshall, *Guy Hocquenghem: Beyond Gay Identity* (Durham, N.C.: Duke University Press, 1997); Julian Bourg, *From Revolution to Ethics: May 1968 and Contemporary French Thought* (Montreal and Kingston: McGill-Queen's Press, 2007), 182–92.
39. René Schérer, *Guy Hocquenghem: La révolte (1946–1988)* (Paris: Éditions de sextant, 2015), 25.
40. Bensaïd, *An Impatient Life,* 277.
41. On the complex relationship between "French Theory" and the American left more generally, see François Cusset, *French Theory: How Foucault, Derrida, Deleuze & Co. Transformed the Intellectual Life of the United States* (Minneapolis: University of Minnesota Press, 2008).
42. As Bensaïd put it, "Latin America was a kind of twin continent in our political imaginary" (Bensaïd, *An Impatient Life,* 95).
43. Ibid., 141.
44. Ibid., 146. Bensaïd noticed the rise of language related to "terrorism," as well as the political productivity of the elasticity of the term as far back as the 1980s (and thus well before the acceleration and proliferation of these trends after September 11, 2001). Reflecting on this later, he wrote: "Every society develops a specific culture of violence. The age of capital and colonial conquests saw what Marx and Engels perceived right away, in relation to the civil war in the United States, as an 'industry of massacre'. Prefiguring what today are called 'humanitarian catastrophes', the colonial genocides and Victorian holocaust were the shadow side of modernity" (ibid., 150)
45. The PRT was founded in 1976 through the merger of two Trotskyist groups (the International Communist League and the Mexican Morenists), later joined by the Marxist Workers' League in 1977. During the 1980s, it was the largest far-left party to challenge the Institutional Revolutionary Party (PRI), until it was eventually eclipsed by the Democratic Revolutionary Party (PRD). It dissolved in 1996.
46. Bensaïd, *An Impatient Life,* 69.

47. Ibid., 210.
48. Enzo Traverso, *Left-Wing Melancholia: Marxism, History, and Memory* (New York: Columbia University Press, 2016), chapter 7 ("Synchronic Times: Walter Benjamin and Daniel Bensaïd"), 204–34, 214.
49. Cinzia Arruzza and Patrick King, "Introduction," *Historical Materialism* 24.4 (2016): 3–8, 3.
50. Bensaïd, *An Impatient Life,* 11.

The Dispossessed

1. Karl Marx, "Debates on Freedom of the Press and Publications of the Proceedings of the Assembly of the Estates," *Rheinische Zeitung,* no. 132, May 12, 1842, Supplement (154–64), specific quotation on 161–62, in *Karl Marx—Frederick Engels Collected Works—Volume 1 (1835–1843),* trans. Clemens Dutt (New York: International Publishers, 1975).
2. Karl Marx, "Justification of the Correspondent from the Mosel," *Rheinische Zeitung,* no. 15, January 15, 1843, 333, in *Karl Marx—Frederick Engels Collected Works—Volume 1 (1835–1843).* [Note that although Bensaïd references an article from 1842 in the original French text, the correct citation is January 15, 1843.—Trans.]
3. Karl Marx, "Justification of the Correspondent from the Mosel," *Rheinische Zeitung,* no. 19, January 19, 1843, 349 in *Karl Marx—Frederick Engels Collected Works—Volume 1 (1835–1843).*
4. Karl Marx, "A Contribution to the Critique of Political Economy (1859)," in *Karl Marx—Frederick Engels Collected Works—Volume 29 (1857–1861),* trans. Yuri Sdobnikov (New York: International Publishers, 1987), 261–62 [emphasis in original].
5. This presentation of the 1842 articles is inspired by Pierre Lascoumes and Hartwig Zander's book *Marx: du "vol de bois" à la critique du droit* (Paris: PUF, 1984), which constitutes an irreplaceable document. On the philosophical turn of 1843–44, see in particular Stathis Kouvélakis, *Philosophie et révolution* (Paris: PUF, 2004) [*Philosophy and Revolution: From Kant to Marx* (New York: Verso, 2003)], and Daniel Bensaïd, "Présentation commentaire critique de *Sur la Question juive*" (Paris: La Fabrique éditions, 2006).
6. Hans Stein, "Karl Marx und der rheinische Pauperismus des Vormärz," in *Jahrbuch des Kölnischen Geschichtsvereins,* no. 14, 1932, 132. [The precise terms of this citation do not appear in the given reference and may be erroneous.—Trans.]
7. [In this section, Bensaïd uses the term "les ayants-droit," a technical term that has no direct equivalent in English. It refers to rights holders who gain their claim on the basis of long-standing use or personal connection, and is variously translated as "beneficiary," "entitlement claimant," etc.—Trans.]
8. Lascoumes and Zander, *Marx,* 104.
9. Karl Marx, *Rheinische Zeitung,* no. 298, October 25, 1842.
10. Ibid.
11. E. P. Thompson, "Mode de domination et révolution en Angleterre," *Actes de la recherche en sciences sociales,* nos. 2–3, 1976, 133–51.

12. Lascoumes and Zander, *Marx,* 108.
13. Karl Marx, "On the Jewish Question," in *Karl Marx—Frederick Engels Collected Works—Volume 3, 1843–1844,* trans. Clemens Dutt (New York: International Publishers, 1975), 146–74.
14. Lascoumes and Zander, *Marx,* 242.
15. Frédéric Zenati, *Essai critique sur la nature juridique de la propriété* (Lyon). [Unpublished material quoted by Lascoumes and Zander.—Trans.]
16. Ernst Bloch, *Droit Naturel et dignité humaine* (Paris: Payot, 1976). [Bensaïd does not provide a precise citation for the passage he is referencing here. However, in the context of a chapter on the "Origin of the State," Bloch does write the following: "The primitive commune of hunter tribes did not need to be attacked by herding tribes in order to become a society of classes. Quite the contrary, the progressive, immanent division of labor itself formed the dominant class, which was ultimately made into something formidable by the state; all progress in the division of labor entailed the transformation of the state into an instrument of domination, but this process was not in the least imposed from without. *Inequality in the ownership of the means of production,* and nothing else, led, in an economically immanent way, to the destruction of tribal solidarity and to the formation of a political class violence" (Ernst Bloch, *Natural Law and Human Dignity,* trans. Dennis J. Schmidt [Cambridge-London: MIT Press, 1986], 270).—Trans.]
17. Karl Polanyi, *La grande transformation.* (Paris: Gallimard, 1972), 115. English edition: *The Great Transformation,* 2d ed. (Boston: Beacon Press, 2001 [1957]), 82.
18. Polanyi, *The Great Transformation,* 86–87.
19. Christine Fauré, *La Déclaration des droits de l'homme de 1789* (Paris: Payot, 1988), 110.
20. [Maximilien de Robespierre, *Recueil des Œuvres de Max. J. Robespierre* (Paris: Revueillis, 1819), vol. II, 398.—Trans.]
21. Outline of the Declaration of Human Rights of April 1793, in Robespierre, *Pour le bonheur et pour la liberté* (Paris: La Fabrique éditions, 2000), 231. [Article 12 of this draft stipulates: "Society is compelled to provide for the sustenance of all its members, either by providing them work, or by providing the means of existence to those who are unable to work." The French Constitution of October 27, 1946, establishes and defends similar rights. For instance, "Everyone shall have the obligation to work and the right to obtain employment. No one may suffer in his work or his employment because of his origin, his opinions or his beliefs . . . The Nation shall guarantee to all, and particularly to the child, the mother, and the aged worker, protection of health, material security, rest, and leisure. Any individual who, because of his or her age, his or her physical or mental condition, or because of the economic situation, shall find himself or herself unable to work, shall have the right to obtain from the community the means for a decent existence" (Preface to the Constitution of the French Republic [1946], trans. French Embassy, Press and Information Division, 610 Fifth Avenue, New York)—Trans.]

22. Daniel Guérin, *La lutte des classes sous la 1e République* (Paris: Gallimard, 1968). English version: *Class Struggle in the First French Republic: Bourgeois and Bras Nus 1793–1795,* trans. Ian Patterson (London: Pluto, 1977).
23. Florence Gauthier and Guy-Robert Ikni, "De Mably à Robespierre," in *La guerre du blé au XVIIIe siècle* (Paris: Éditions de la Passion, 1988). [This collection of articles contains an important essay by E. P. Thompson: "The Moral Economy of the English Crowd in the Eighteenth Century," originally published in the review *Past & Present,* no. 50 (February 1971): 76–136.—Trans.]
24. Gauthier and Ikni, "De Mably à Roberpierre," 19.
25. Alexis de Tocqueville, *Souvenirs* (Paris: Folio–Gallimard, 1978), 48. English version: *The Recollections of Alexis de Tocqueville,* trans. Alexander Teixeira de Mattos (New York: Macmillan, 1896), 13; new edition: *Recollections: The French Revolution of 1848 and Its Aftermath,* ed. Oliver Zunz, trans. Arthur Goldhammer (Charlottesville: University of Virginia Press, 2016).
26. Marx, *Rheinische Zeitung,* no. 298, October 25, 1842. Marx later adds in the same article published in the *Rheinische Zeitung,* no. 300, dated October 27, 1842: "In these customs of the poor class, therefore, there is an instinctive sense of right; their roots are positive and legitimate, and the form of *customary right* here conforms all the more to nature because up to now the *existence of the poor class itself* has been a *mere custom* of civil society, a custom that has not found an appropriate place in the conscious organization of the state."
27. The label *Levellers* appeared during the agrarian revolts in 1607. It then designated the radical egalitarian wing of the English revolution of 1647–53. The Levellers found their main support among artisans, shopkeepers, simple soldiers, and independent workers. In the nineteenth century, the word served to stigmatize "communists, reds, sharers."
28. See C. B. Macpherson, *The Political Theory of Possessive Individualism: Hobbes to Locke* (Oxford: Oxford University Press, 1990), 139–40 and 276–77.
29. ["The Putney Debates," in Sir William Clarke, *Puritanism and Liberty, being the Army Debates (1647–9) from the Clarke Manuscripts with Supplementary Documents,* selected and edited with an Introduction by A. S. P. Woodhouse (Chicago: University of Chicago Press, 1951), 69.—Trans.]
30. [Ibid., 71.—Trans.]
31. Concerning the Levellers, see Olivier Lutaud's *Les Niveleurs, Cromwell et la République* (Paris:, Archives Julliard, 1967), and Christopher Hill, *La Révolution anglaise 1640* (Paris: Éditions de la Passion, 1993). [Christopher Hill, *The English Revolution* (London: Lawrence & Wishart, 1959).] [This section contains a number of quotes, which appear to be paraphrases from various sections from Lutaud and Hill. No precise page numbers are given by Bensaïd.—Trans.]
32. Thomas Hobbes, *Leviathan* (Paris: Folio–Gallimard, 2000 [1651]), 297, 383, 482. See also Thomas Hobbes, *Leviathan,* ed. J. C. A. Gaskin (Oxford: Oxford University Press, 1998), 119, 164, 215.
33. G. W. F. Hegel, *Elements of the Philosophy of Right,* ed. Allen W. Wood, trans. H. B. Nisbet (Cambridge: Cambridge University Press, 1991), §127 and

128. One can find in French law a resonance to this right of necessity under the label of "necessity-right" *(droit de nécessité).*

34. Ibid., §100. This paragraph makes explicit reference to §75: "The nature of the state has just as little to do with the relationship of contract, whether it is assumed that the state is a contract of all with all, or a contract of all with the sovereign and the government.—The intrusion of this relationship, and of relationships concerning private property in general, into political relationships has created the greatest confusion in constitutional law [Staatsrecht] and in actuality. Just as in earlier times political rights and duties were regarded as, and declared to be, the immediate private property of particular individuals in opposition to the right of the sovereign and the state, so also in more recent times have the rights of the sovereign and the state been regarded as objects of contract and based on a contract, as the result merely of a common will and proceeding from the arbitrary will of those who have combined to form a state.—However different these two points of view may be in one respect, they do have this in common: they have transferred the determinations of private property to a sphere of a totally different and higher nature."
35. [Bensaïd is quoting from Marx's article from November 1, 1842, *Rheinische Zeitung,* no. 305.—Trans.]
36. A new, posthumous essay by Proudhon appeared in 1866, *The Theory of Property,* in which he exposes an irreconcilable opposition between communal right and private property from a study of the Slavic, Germanic, and Arab societies.
37. [The *sans-culottes* were lower-class radicals who composed the majority of revolutionary army (so named for their poor clothing, specifically, their lack of knee breeches *(culottes)* favored by the upper classes).—Trans.]
38. [Marie Joseph Louis Adolphe Thiers was a French politician and historian. He was the second elected president of France and first president of the Third Republic.—Trans.]
39. [Named for the eleventh month of the French Republican calendar (Thermidor), the Thermidorians were a political faction in revolutionary France. Led by Paul Barras, Jean-Lambert Tallien, and Jospeh Fouché, they deposed Robespierre and Saint-Just in 1794 and ruled France until 1799 when Napoleon Bonaparte removed them from power via the coup of the 18 Brumaire.—Trans.]
40. Jean-Jacques Rousseau, *Discours sur l'origine et les fondements de l'inégalité parmi les hommes* (Paris: Garnier-Flammarion, 1971), 220; Jean-Jacques Rousseau, *Discourse on the Origin of Inequality,* trans. Donald A. Cress (Indianapolis: Hackett Publishing, 1992), 44–45.
41. Rousseau, *Discours sur l'origine et les fondements de l'inégalité parmi les hommes,* 225; Rousseau, *Discourse on the Origin of Inequality,* 62.
42. Pierre-Joseph Proudhon, *Qu'est-ce que la propriété?* (Paris: Garnier Flammarion, 1966), 120, 265. English translation: *What Is Property?,* trans. Donald R. Kelley and Bonnie G. Smith (Cambridge: Cambridge University Press, 1994), 66, 178.
43. John Locke, *Traité du gouvernement civil* (Paris: Garnier Flammarion,

1984), 195–96. Quotation taken from the original English text: *Two Treatises of Government,* ed. Peter Laslett (Cambridge: Cambridge University Press, 1988), 287–88.

44. Proudhon, *Qu'est-ce que la propriété?,* 129; Proudhon, *What Is Property?,* 69. [Bensaïd's citations are in fact a collage of different passages found in these sections of Proudhon's text.—Trans.]
45. Proudhon, *What Is Property?,* 43 and 140.
46. Proudhon, *Qu'est-ce que la propriété?,* 148; Proudhon, *What Is Property?,* 85.
47. Proudhon, *Qu'est-ce que la propriété?,* 141; Proudhon, *What Is Property?,* 79.
48. Proudhon, *Qu'est-ce que la propriété?,* 149; Proudhon, *What Is Property?,* 86.
49. Paul Sereni, *Marx, la personne et la chose* (Paris: L'Harmattan, 2007), 43 and 60.
50. In a letter dated January 24, 1865, addressed to J. B. von Schweitzer and edited by the *Sozial-Demokrat,* Marx maintains his initial eulogistic judgment on *What Is Property?* This work by Proudhon is "undoubtedly his best. It is epoch-making, if not because of the novelty of its content, at least because of the new and audacious way of expressing old ideas." The style of the essay is its great achievement: "a deep and genuine feeling of indignation at the infamy of the existing order, a revolutionary earnestness—all these electrified the readers of *Qu'est-ce que la propriété?* and provided a strong stimulus on its first appearance" (Karl Marx, "On Proudhon" [Letter to J. B. von Schweitzer], London, January 24, 1865, *Sozial-Demokrat,* no. 16, February 1, 1865, in *Marx & Engels, Collected Works. Volume 20, 1864–1868* [New York: International Publishers, 1985], 26–27).
51. Pierre-Joseph Proudhon, *Philosophie de la misère* (Paris: Union générale d'éditions [UGE], 10–18, 1964), 217; Pierre-Joseph Proudhon, *System of Economical Contradictions, or The Philosophy of Misery,* trans. Benjamin R. Tucker (Benj. R. Tucker: Boston, 1888, repr. New York: Arno Press, 1972). [This passage is taken from one of the two last chapters of Proudhon's essay titled "Huitième époque—La propriété" that is absent from any English translation I have found in a published form or that I could consult online. Even the most recent English publication of Proudhon's *Philosophy of Poverty* (2015) does not include the three last chapters of the French original edition.—Trans.]
52. Karl Marx, *Misère de la philosophie* (Paris: UGE, 10–18, 1964), 304; Karl Marx, "The Poverty of Philosophy," in *Karl Marx and Frederick Engels Collected Works—Volume 6 (1845–1848)* (London: Lawrence & Wishart, 2010), 134. [Translation modified.—Trans.]
53. Proudhon, *Philosophie de la misère,* 304. [See explanatory note re: missing passages in the standard English translation at footnote 51.—Trans.]
54. Marx, *Misère de la philosophie,* 361, 369, 401; Marx, "The Poverty of Philosophy," 137, 143, 159.
55. [Marx, "The Poverty of Philosophy," 132.—Trans.]
56. Proudhon, *Philosophie de la misère,* 430.
57. [Marx, "The Poverty of Philosophy," 211.—Trans.]
58. Karl Marx and Friedrich Engels, *Correspondance,* vol. 7 (Paris: Éditions sociales, 1979), 12–13; English version: Karl Marx, "On Proudhon" [Letter to

J. B. von Schweitzer], London, January 24, 1865, *Sozial-Demokrat,* nos. 16, 17, and 18 in February 1, 3, and 5, 1865. In *Marx & Engels, Collected Works. Volume 20, 1864–1868,* 27, 28, 29.

59. Paul Sereni asks how Marx can talk about theft and looting without referring to a normative theory of justice. If the law is intrinsically bourgeois, as *The Critique of the Gotha Program* asserts, would there be a metalegal norm, or the only prospect of the decline of the law?
60. Jean Peyrelevade, *Le capitalisme total* (Paris: Seuil, "La République des Idées," 2005), 42. *Forbes* magazine's annual rankings list 415 billionaires (in dollars) in 2006. Less than a thousand people hold $3,500 billion, double the gross domestic product of France. Between 1966 and 2001, the income of the richest 10 percent increased by 58 percent, the income of the richest 1 percent by 236 percent, and that of the richest 0.01 percent by 617 percent. Two percent of the world's population owns half of the financial assets, while 50 percent of the poorest share 1 percent. In one year, the wealth of the four hundred richest Americans has grown by $120 billion. Casino mogul Sheldon Adelson has cashed in one million dollars per hour since 2004. The average American earning the median salary is expected to work twenty-nine thousand years to join the *Forbes* ranking. In the late 1990s, a UNCTAD (United Nations Conference on Trade and Development) report found that some one hundred companies are "redrawing the world." They alone held $1,800 billion abroad, employed six million workers worldwide, and had annual sales of $2,100 billion. By way of comparison, UN experts estimate that twenty-five billion dollars over ten years will be needed to provide drinking water for the 1.5 billion people who lack it, and about ten billion dollars for the budget needed for the fight against AIDS in Africa.
61. The General Agreement on Trade and Services covers thirteen sectors subdivided into 163 subsectors concerning finance, recreation, sports, education, environment, distribution, communication, and "others."
62. Daniel Cohen, *Trois leçons sur la société postindustrielle* (Paris: Seuil, "La République des Idées," 2006), 69; English edition: *Three Lectures on Postindustrial Society,* trans. William McCuaig (Cambridge: MIT Press, 2009). [Exact English equivalent not found.—Trans.]
63. Ibid.
64. Dominique Pestre, "À propos du nouveau régime de production, d'appropriation et de régulation des savoirs," *Contretemps,* no. 14 (Paris: Textuel, September 2005).
65. See Alain Sokal, "Science et marché des savoirs," *Contretemps,* no. 14. When the Sarkozyist minister of universities, Valérie Pécresse, sums up the spirit of her reform by announcing "the idea of giving French universities a setup better adapted to the world in which we live," this is also what it is all about. And because this world of forced commodification has its own logic, it is necessary "that universities can freely manage their real estate, freely recruit the teachers they want, manage their credits as they see fit" (*Journal du dimanche,* May 27, 2007). This is quite simply a declaration of the opening of the educational market to competition.

66. Grégoire Chamayou, "Le débat américain sur liberté, innovation, domaine public," *Contretemps*, no. 5 (Paris: Textuel, 2002). This article presents an excellent critical synthesis of the controversy on intellectual property and its philosophical presuppositions.
67. Karl Marx, "A Contribution to the Critique of Political Economy" (1859), in *Karl Marx—Frederick Engels Collected Works—Volume 28 (1857–1861)*, 509; trans. Ernst Wangerman (London: Lawrence & Wishart, digital edition, 2010); and Karl Marx, "A Contribution to the Critique of Political Economy" (1859), in *Karl Marx—Frederick Engels Collected Works—Volume 29 (1857–1861)*, 90–91, trans. Viktor Schnittke (New York: International Publishers, 1987).
68. "Would it not be criminal, asks Proudhon, if some islanders were to repulse, in the name of property, the unfortunate victims of a shipwreck trying to reach the shore?" (*What Is Property?*, trans. Donald R. Kelley and Bonnie G. Smith [Cambridge: Cambridge University Press, 1994], 47.) Nowadays, this has nevertheless become a daily part of the world's miseries, in Ceuta and Melilla, on the Italian coasts, or on the border of the Rio Grande.
69. Article 5, Directive 98/44/EC of the European Parliament and of the Council of July 6, 1998, on the Legal Protection of biotechnological inventions.
70. Illustrating the emergence of a *g-business* (g as gene), no less than twenty-eight biotechnology companies went public in the summer of 2000, including nine in Europe.
71. [These are categories used by Marx. For instance, most famously in chapter 10 of *Capital*, vol. 1, Marx defines Capital as "dead labour which, vampire-like, lives only by sucking living labour, and lives the more, the more labour it sucks" (*Capital*, vol. 1 [New York: Penguin, 1990]).—Trans.]
72. Daniel Cohen, "La propriété intellectuelle, c'est le vol" [Intellectual property is theft], *Le Monde*, April 8, 2001: http://www.lemonde.fr/archives/article/2001/04/08/la-propriete-intellectuelle-c-est-le-vol_4175020_1819218.html?xtmc=&xtcr=1.>.
73. Joseph Stiglitz, "Le libre accès au savoir tient du bien public mondial" [Free access to knowledge is global public good], interview with Christian Lansson, *Libération*, September 13, 2006: http://www.liberation.fr/futurs/2006/09/13/le-libre-acces-au-savoir-tient-du-bien-public-mondial_51119>.
74. On Christmas Eve 2005, an almost empty French parliament voted by a two-vote majority to amend legislation on all types of downloading. A step seemed to have been taken toward "the global license." The law of March 2006 on copyright and related rights in the information society (DADVSI) imposes penalties on illegal downloading on the Internet and prohibits copies for private use. Yet it is the absence of patents that allowed the initial rise of the Internet and the proliferation of creativity that followed. Intellectual property is indeed shaking up new technologies that are themselves the fruit of highly socialized work. If software is "information that deals with information," it is the product of interactive collective creation.
75. James Boyle, "The Second Enclosure Movement and the Construction of

the Public Domain," *Law and Contemporary Problems* 66.33 (Durham, N.C.: Duke University School of Law, winter/spring 2003): 50: "Once a new intellectual property right has been created over some informational good, the only way to ensure efficient allocation of that good is to give the rights holder still greater control over the user or consumer in the aftermarket so as to allow for price discrimination, since the only efficient monopoly is a monopoly with perfect price discrimination." On these issues, also see the review *Contretemps*, no. 5 (September 2002): "Propriété et Pouvoir."

76. Between 1993 and 2005, IBM filed more patents than any other company in the United States (twenty-six thousand in the United States and more than forty thousand worldwide).
77. Olivier Ezratty, quoted in "Une arme à double tranchant pour les entreprises," *Le Monde Interactif*, November 15, 2000, 111.
78. One of the concerns with these forms of social appropriation of culture and knowledge pertains to the remuneration of researchers or authors. In the terms of competitive ideology and the race for profit, the question confuses the legitimate right to a guaranteed income with a right to private property and rent. In fact, the right to income poses the general problem of its increased socialization, in relation to the socialization of work itself, in other words an extension of wages at work in today's social protection systems.
79. [L'Assemblée Mondiale des Élus et Citoyens pour l'Eau (AMECE) was a conference of dozens of national and international organizations that took place at the European Parliament in Brussels in 2007. It was a continuation of the first Forum Alternatif Mondial de l'Eau (FAME), which was held in 2003 in Florence.—Trans.]
80. Proudhon, *Qu'est-ce que la propriété?*, 130; Proudhon, *What Is Property?*, 70–71.
81. See Mike Davis, *Planet of Slums* (New York: Verso, 2006).
82. Proudhon, *Qu'est-ce que la propriété?*, 157, 176, 228; Proudhon, *What Is Property?*, 94, 111, 113, 114, 150.
83. David Harvey, *Spaces of Global Capitalism* (London: Verso, 2006), 45.
84. [A phrase associated with the work of Hannah Arendt. For recent analysis and commentary, see Stephanie DeGooyer, Alastair Hunt, Lida Maxwell, Samuel Moyn, and Astra Taylor, *The Right to Have Rights* (New York: Verso, 2018).—Trans.]
85. [On this topic, see my *Theft Is Property! Dispossession and Critical Theory* (Durham, N.C.: Duke University Press, 2020).—Trans.]
86. [E.g., "The tradition of the oppressed teaches us that the 'state of emergency' in which we live is not the exception but the rule" (Walter Benjamin, "Theses on the Philosophy of History," in *Illuminations*, ed. Hannah Arendt. (New York: Schocken Books, 1968), 257.—Trans.]
87. "(1) Abolition of property in land and application of all rents of land to public purposes. (2) A heavy progressive or graduated income tax. (3) Abolition of all right of inheritance. (4) Confiscation of the property of all emigrants and rebels. (5) Centralisation of credit in the hands of the State, by means of a national bank with State capital and an exclusive monopoly.

(6) Centralisation of the means of communication and transport in the hands of the State. (7) Extension of factories and instruments of production owned by the State; the bringing into cultivation of waste-lands, and the improvement of the soil generally in accordance with a common plan" (Karl Marx—Frederick Engels, "Manifesto of the Communist Party," in *Karl Marx—Friedrich Engels Collected Works—Volume 6 (1845–1848)*, 505).

88. Karl Marx, *Capital: A Critique of Political Economy*, vol. 1, trans. Ben Fowkes, chapter 32: "The Historical Tendency of Capitalist Accumulation" (Harmondsworth: Penguin Books, 1976), 929.
89. [The term for public land under Roman law.—Trans.]
90. Karl Marx, "Comments on James Mill, *Éléments d'économie politique*," in *Karl Marx—Frederick Engels Collected Works—Volume 3 (1843–1844)*, 227–28.
91. Sereni, *Marx, la personne et la chose*, 209 and 219. Sereni disputes Engels's reading, too narrow in his opinion, that Marx's text would suggest only a distinction between the *social* ownership of the means of production versus *individual* ownership of products and objects of consumption. In *Homo aequalis* (Paris: Gallimard, 1977), Louis Dumont develops an interpretation of Marx as a consistent egalitarian liberal that goes in a similar direction.
92. This is notably the subject of Antoine Artous's book *Le Fétichisme chez Marx* (Paris: Syllepse, 2006), and his critical reviews by Stavros Tombazos in *Contretemps*, nos. 20 and 21, 5
93. Sereni, *Marx, la personne et la chose*. [No precise citation found.—Trans.]
94. See Jean Sylvestre, "Les progiciels de la micro-informatique comme modèle de rente" [The computer software package as an annuity model], *Contretemps*, no. 5 (Paris: Textuel, 2002).
95. Rifkin, false prophet that he is, noted in 2000 that thirty million Americans were already living in areas of Common Interest Development (CID), that is, in residential compounds for wealthy people who confiscated public space: "Since CIDs have no 'public space,' they do not have to open their communities to the public." It's difficult to see in this privatization of the street and space a decline of private property rather than its extension to the city and to life! [See Jeremy Rifkin, *The Age of Access* (New York: Putnam, 2000), 122.]
96. Laurent Fabius in *La Revue socialiste*, no.1 (spring 1999).
97. From Marx to Blum, through Blanqui, Guesde, and Jaurès, all knew very well that "property is power." By yielding on this point, liberal socialists paved the way for their future electoral failures. The political scientist Zaki Laïdi even welcomed the fact that Jospin allegedly "privatized more than Juppé." He even stated jubilantly, "because ownership is no longer essential," and "the rise of pension funds in the financial regulation is there to emphasize that the hardening of competition is not incompatible with the development of a popular capitalism." For this triumphant march of markets, public property would instead become a "handicap to the mobilization of resources" and would inevitably "disappear from the regulation of market relations" (Zaki Laïdi, *Le Monde*, September 1, 1998).
98. Milton Friedman, "La 'troisième voie' est sans issue," *Le Monde* (July 20, 1999).

99. Sociologist Anthony Giddens has been the ideologue for Blairism and its "Third Way" through the publication of an eponymous book-manifesto. Bodo Hombart played an equivalent role in Germany through Gerhart Schroeder with his New Center theory (Neues Zentrum).
100. [Founded in November 2006, Les Enfants de Don Quichotte [Don Quixote's Children] is a French social justice organization primarily concerned with combating homelessness and defending the right to habitation. See Patrick Bruneteaux, ed., *Les Enfants de Don Quichotte: Sociologie d'une improbable mobilization nationale* (Paris: Presses universitaires de Vincennes, 2013).—Trans.]
101. [Nicolas Hulot (born 1955) is a French politician and environmental activist. He served as French minister of the environment in 2017–18. See Nicolas Hulot, *Pour un pacte écologique* (Paris: Calmann-Lévy, 2006).—Trans.]
102. [The CAC 40 is a benchmark French stock-market index.—Trans.]
103. See Daniel Tanuro's articles on europe-solidaire.org and his interview with Jean-Pascal van Ypersele in *Inprecor*, no. 525 (February–March 2007).
104. This is one of the reasons why research on the capabilities of photovoltaic cells hasn't been faster. Studies published in 2006, however, state that photovoltaic cells would experimentally achieve 40 percent conversion of solar energy into electrical energy (instead of 20 percent previously).
105. [The Association pour la Taxation des Transactions Financières et l'Aide aux Citoyens (Attac) is a network of "alter-globalization" organizations originally founded in France in 1999. See https://www.attac.org/en.—Trans.]
106. ["Differentialism" is a far-right political and intellectual movement that asserts the essential and incommensurable differences between social groups, characterized variously in cultural, ethnic, or biological terms. It is associated with the "New Right" *(Nouvelle Droite)* in France, but especially Alain de Benoist and his Groupement de recherche et d'études pour la civilisation européenne.—Trans.]
107. Chamayou, "Le débat américain liberté, innovation, domaine public," 49.
108. ["Nos vies valent mieux que leurs profits" was the slogan used by Olivier Besancenot, candidate for the French presidency in 2002 for the Ligue Communiste Révolutionnaire (LCR). The LCR was a Trotskyist political party and French section of the Fourth International, active from 1974 until 2009, when it was folded into the Nouveau Parti Anticapitaliste (NPR). In 1966, Bensaïd was a founding member (along with Alain Krivine) of the LCR's forerunner, the Jeunesse Communiste Révolutionnaire. He was considered a major intellectual voice for the JCR, the LCR, and the NPR alike (connected to Henri Weber), often writing in *La gauche* (Quebec, associated with the Fourth International) and via pamphlets and manifestos of the NPR, such as *Penser Agir: pour un gauche anticapitaliste* [Think, Act: For an anticapitalist Left] and *Prenons parti: pour un socialisme du XXIe siècle* [Let's take part/take advantage: for a twenty-first century socialism] (coauthored with Olivier Besancenot). See "Crisis and Kleptocracy" at beginning of this book for more details.—Trans.]

Proceedings of the Sixth Rhine Province Assembly, Third Article

1. We regret that we have not been able to publish the second article for our readers. Editorial Board of the *Rheinische Zeitung.*
2. [Genre paintings or genre scenes *[Genrebilder]* are a form of art concerned with representing ordinary people engaged in everyday activities.—Trans.]
3. ["In fact, it is a draft proposal *[proposition de loi]* and not a bill *[projet de loi]*. The draft was prepared within the state apparatus in accordance with its legislative powers. It could be solicited by petitions from cities or provincial assemblies. The bill was subsequently presented to the provincial assemblies by the State Ministry, on the orders of the king."—D.B.]
4. [In Bensaïd's appendix, he has added a footnote that the word in the original *Rheinische Zeitung* article is *negokryphisch,* but that he has corrected this to *apocryphal,* "following the suggestion proposed by Mehring." I have not been able to find the correction to which Bensaïd is referring (presumably by Franz Mehring), but do note that in the *Marx–Engels Gesamtausgabe,* the word is *negokryphisch.* See *Matx–Engels Gesamtausgabe,* Erste Abteilung, Band I (Berlin: Dietz Verlag, 1975), 199.—Trans.]
5. [As far as I have been able to determine, all quotes on the parliamentary debates are from *Sitzungs-Protokolle des sechsten Rheinischen Provinzial-Landtags* (Koblenz, 1841).—Trans.]
6. [A reference to the Criminal Code of Karl V: *Die peinliche Halsgerichtsordnung Kaiser Karls V. Constitutio criminalis Carolina* (1532).—Trans.]
7. [This point is made by Bensaïd in Part I, "'Rural Pauperism' and 'Forest Malfeasance.'"—Trans.]
8. Montesquieu, *The Spirit of the Laws* (Cambridge: Cambridge University Press, 1989), Part I, Book 6, Chapter XII, 86. "Il y a deux genres de corruption," says Montesquieu, "l'un lorsque le people n'observe point les lois; l'autre lorsqu'il est corrompu par les lois: mal incurable parce qu'il est dans le remède même" (Montesquieu, *De l'esprit des lois,* tome premier, livre sixième, chapitre XII. [Marx quotes the original French.—Trans.]
9. [Quoted by Bensaïd in Part I, "'Rural Pauperism' and 'Forest Malfeasance.'" —Trans.]
10. [A pun on the German word *Kasten,* meaning both "castes" and "boxes." —Trans.]
11. [Sie werden daher auch nur verlangt als Domänen für die menus plaisirs, damit derselbe Inhalt, der im Gesetz nach seinen vernünftigen Grenzen behandelt ist, in der Gewohnheit einen Spielraum für die Grillen und Anmaßungen wider seine vernünftigen Grenzen finde. "Spielraum für die Grillen"—room for fun? For lofty ideas (i.e., Grillen im Kopt haben)? —Trans.]
12. [The *leges barbarorum* was a Latin compendium of "barbaric laws": a collection of the common law of various Germanic tribes from the fifth to the ninth centuries.—Trans.]
13. ["Here the term *Vergehen* [offense] has been translated well as a *contravention.* We assume from the lexical context that Marx used this term not

in its strict legal sense, but in the more generic sense that also exists in German."—D.B.]

14. [A pun relating the German words *Hühneraugen* (corns) and *Augen* (eyes).—Trans.]
15. [William Shakespeare, *The Merchant of Venice,* Act IV, Scene 1.—Trans.]
16. ["When he is afraid, he is terrible."—Trans.]
17. [In the Bensaïd appendix, after this point the remainder of the article has been edited out. It is reproduced here in its entirety.—Trans.]
18. [In the Bensaïd appendix, after this point the remainder of the article has been edited out. It is reproduced here in its entirety.—Trans.]
19. [Dodona was a town in Epirus, northern Greece. Oracles were said to interpret the will of the gods there by listening to the rustling of leaves from an oak tree planted at the temple of Zeus.—Trans.]
20. ["Nothing is more terrible than logic carried to absurdity."—Trans.]
21. [The quote is from Johann Wolfgang von Goethe, *Reineke Fuchs,* Sechster Gesang. The original lines cited by Marx are "Und es hatte sich Reineke ängstlich und traurig gebärdet, / Daß er manchen gutmütigen Mann zum Mitleid bewegte, / Lampe, der Hase, besonders war sehr bekümmert." The English translation inserted by Clemens Palme Dutt into his edition is "Reineke had been anxious and sad, / Which excited the pity of many a good-natured man, / Lampe, the hare, especially was very distressed." Here, I have added the lines directly from Johann Wolfgang von Goethe, *The Story of Reynard the Fox,* trans. Thomas James Arnold (New York: Heritage Press, 1954), 105.—Trans.]
22. [In the appendix to Bensaïd's work, *Les Dépossédés,* this article has been significantly edited for length. The entirety of the original German text is reproduced here.—Trans.]
23. ["What, at a ball, we simple folk call being wallflowers." A reference to Evariste Parny, "La guerre des dieux anciens et modernes."—Trans.]
24. [A reference to William Shakespeare, *Richard III,* Act V, Scene 4: "A horse, a horse! My kingdom for a horse!"—Trans.]
25. [Feudal or, more precisely, seigniorial right.—Trans.]
26. [In the appendix to Bensaïd's work, *Les Dépossédés,* this article has been significantly edited for length. The entirety of the original German text is reproduced here.—Trans.]
27. ["Divide and conquer."—Trans.]
28. [William Shakespeare, *The Merchant of Venice,* Act IV, Scene 1.—Trans.]
29. [A reference to events during the Spanish siege of Antwerp (1584–85).—Trans.]
30. [A reference to the Nominated Assembly and the Parliament of Saints, also known as the Barebone's or Little Parliament. Assembled by Oliver Cromwell in 1653, it was the last Parliament to meet before Cromwell was made Lord Protector.—Trans.]
31. [Man sucht das Recht gleichsam durch den Terrorismus und die Akkuratesse, die man ihm gegen den Feind gestattet, zu entschädigen für die schlüpfrige Gewissensweitheit, mit der man es als Garantie des Angeklagten und als selbständigen Gegenstand behandelt.—Trans.]

32. [Tidong is a region in Kalimantan, part of what is now Borneo.—Trans.]
33. [The Bensaïd version begins here.—Trans.]
34. ["Marx is making an allusion here to another debate of the Province Assembly regarding a different draft bill related to hunting offenses."—D.B.]

Index

Daniel Bensaïd (1946–2010) was a French philosopher, political activist, and one of the most important Marxist public intellectuals of his generation. He was a founding member of le Mouvement du 22 Mars and Ligue Communiste, and he was active in the Fourth International. His many books include *Marx for Our Times* and *An Impatient Life.*

Robert Nichols is associate professor of political theory in the Department of Political Science at the University of Minnesota. He is author of *Theft Is Property! Dispossession and Critical Theory* and *The World of Freedom: Heidegger, Foucault, and the Politics of Historical Ontology.*